Vital Skills

Study Strategies Every Nursing Student Must Know

Kathleen C. Straker, M.Ed.

Eugenia G. Kelman, Ph.D.

Karista Press
Houston, TX

Karista Press
info@vitalstudyskills.com

ISBN: 978-0-9798475-0-9

Straker, Kathleen C.
    Vital skills : study strategies every nursing student must know / Kathleen C. Straker, M.Ed, Eugenia G. Kelman, Ph.D.
    p. cm.
    ISBN 978-0-9798475-0-9
1. Nursing—Study and teaching. 2. Study skills. 3. Education, Nursing. 4. Students, Nursing. I. Kelman, Eugenia. II. Title.

RT73 .S775 2007
610.73071—dc22   2007906222

Book Production Team
Rita Mills of The Book Connection — Project Manager
www.BookConnectionOnline.com
Gladys Ramirez — Cover Design & Figures
Deborah Frontiera — Line Editing
Nil Santana — Logo Design
Tammy Dubinsky — Illustrations

The paper used in this publication meets the requirements of the American National Standard for Permanence of Paper for Printed Library Materials Z39.48-1984.

Printed in the United States of America

Dedication

To Mom.
You taught me to love to learn.

—KCS

Acknowledgments

From the initial idea to the finished book, we have enjoyed the support and assistance of so many people. We are grateful to —

- Dr. Ronald Johnson and Dr. Faun Ryser for getting the study strategies workshops for nursing students started.

- Dr. Theresa Carroll, Dr. Lene Symes, Dr. Lillian Bernard, Ms. Margie Bentch Landson, Dr. Immaculata Igbo and Ms. Lisa Hughes, with whom we have worked over the past several years.

- Patsy Cannon, MLS; Pamela Friesen, PhD, RN; Carol Haaga, BS, RN; Joyce Haley, MS; Immaculata Igbo, PhD; Margie Bentch Landson, MSN, RN; Carolyn Lewis, PhD, RN, CNE; Tony Moore, CPT; Janie Perez, MA, RN, PNP; Jackie Perry, BSN, RN; Laura DeBow-Platt, RN; Faun Ryser, PhD, RN, CNS; Shirley D. Straker, MA and Elizabeth Treece, BS, RDH, for reviewing and commenting on drafts of this manuscript. Your comments and insights were invaluable and helped make this a better book. We, of course, take responsibility for any mistakes that may remain.

- D. Griffith, BSN, RN; R. Mistry, BS, RN and L. DeBow-Platt, RN for letting us include their study notes as examples in this book.

- The students who have attended our workshops and shared a portion of their journey with us.

It has been a joy to know and work with you all!

Table of Contents

List of Figures, Worksheets, Tables, Charts

Foreword

Don't let the size fool you. This little book is absolutely crammed full of the best study strategies and self-help information a person could ever want or need. It is relevant, to-the-point and an easy read. The exercises are quick, simple and revealing. The tools and worksheets provided are easy to use. No wasted time here.

I would recommend this book to students at every level of education even if they are *not* nursing students.

A big "thank you" to Kathleen Straker and Jean Kelman for providing tools to help students comprehend complex material and develop efficient study habits.

Laura M. DeBow-Platt, RN
Texas Children's Hospital
Houston, Texas

———————

You may have heard the saying, "I used to be an 'A' student. Now I'm a nursing student."

But it doesn't have to be true!

It takes a lot of hard work and good grades to be accepted to a nursing program. But even that does not fully prepare you for the tremendous work load and course content. Many nursing students feel overwhelmed.

I was introduced to the *Vital Skills* study system during my first semester of nursing school at Texas Woman's University.

Eureka!

This program provided me with skills that not only saved time, but also increased my productivity and test scores. Most importantly, this study system gave me breathing space. Confidence in my knowledge of the material increased exponentially, especially while preparing for the NCLEX.

Now is a good time to take inventory of your study skills, test taking skills and time management. *Vital Skills* will help you identify areas that need improvement and give you some smart and simple strategies for learning.

Vital Skills helped me succeed in nursing school and it can help you, too.

Carol Haaga, BS, RN
The Methodist Hospital
Houston, Texas

Vital Skills

An Introduction to This Workbook

> *Learning is one-third smarts and two-thirds sweat.*

Congratulations!
If you are considering a nursing degree,
you have selected an excellent career opportunity!

What Makes Nursing an Outstanding Career?

Nurses are needed now. Though there are about two and a half million nurses in the U.S., there is still a serious shortage. Wherever you might want to live, there are jobs available for nurses. And more nursing jobs will be created in the future than for any other occupation, according to the U.S. Department of Labor. Opportunities are not just available, they abound!

Nurses also enjoy their choice of work setting, depending on their special interests and training. They can work in hospitals (three out of five nurses do), in medical offices, as home health care providers, in public health departments, school environments, industry and many other settings.

Working conditions are good, and nurses usually enjoy excellent benefits in addition to respectable salaries. *The Occupational Outlook Handbook* reports that most nurses earn in the $40,000 to $60,000 range per year, plus benefits that usually are valued at about one-third of salary. Nurses who have specialized training, such as nurse practitioners or nurse anesthetists, earn considerably more.

In addition to the tangible advantages of this career, nurses are respected members of the community. They enjoy the satisfaction of knowing they provide vitally necessary help to others. Nurses do more than offer "tender loving care" (TLC) to patients, they also assist in disease prevention and health promotion as nurse educators, researchers, and public health employees.

Nurses Must Be Competent As Well As Caring

Like most professional work, entering a career in nursing involves some challenges, including acquiring specialized skills and knowledge. Nurses must graduate from an approved nursing program, pass a national licensing examination and be licensed in the state where they work.

(If you are already enrolled in a nursing program, you may skip the next two headings and resume reading at the section entitled "Nursing Program Requirements, page 4.")

Three Types of Nursing Programs

There are three types of nursing education programs that lead to becoming a Registered Nurse (RN):

1. Colleges and universities offer bachelor degrees in nursing, usually the Bachelor of Science in Nursing (BSN). At the last count there were 678 such programs in the United States. Typically, students entering bachelor's programs have already completed two years as undergraduates in a college or university. They then take two to two-and-a-half more years of courses at a university nursing program.

2. Community colleges and junior colleges offer the associates degree in nursing (ADN). These programs take two to three years to complete. There are about 700 ADN programs in the United States.

3. Diploma programs are still offered by some hospitals. They usually require three years to complete. Only about 100 diploma programs currently exist in the U.S.

The All Nursing Schools website (www.allnursing schools.com) has information comparing these three options.

Factors to Consider When Choosing a Nursing Program

Though all three programs are approved educational paths to an entry-level position as a nurse, the BSN degree is most favored in the profession and will usually lead to more rapid advancement or to supervisory positions. If, however, you have parental responsibilities, work to support yourself and your family while you attend school, or have other time-consuming commitments, you may find that an ADN program permitting part-time attendance, will best fit your needs. As you will learn in the chapter on time management, full-time attendance at a nursing school is a full-time job, requiring between forty and forty-five hours a week, possibly more if your pre-nursing education did not provide a strong background.

Nursing Program Requirements

The typical nursing student has about fifteen contact hours (or fifteen credit hours) per term. That means being in class or in related activities fifteen or more hours a week. A reasonable calculation of study time is one-and-a-half to two hours for each credit hour. Some courses may require less; whereas others may demand more of your time, depending on course content and your earlier preparation. This means that a full-time baccalaureate program will easily require 40-45 hours per week of lectures, clinical work and personal study.

About one-third of nurses currently have a BSN degree, but the National Advisory Council on Nurse Education and Practice (NACNEP) recommends that by 2010, at least two-thirds of all RNs have BSN degrees. Because of their competitive nature, graduate level programs require strong undergraduate preparation.

Nursing courses cover scientific subjects where just attending the lecture or reading the book will not lead to passing tests or to long-term retention. You must not only remember detailed information, but also be able to apply it in order to pass the exams. Instead of cramming information just to pass one test, nursing students need to commit the material to long-term memory. You must be able to recall and apply the information later in the same course, when you take other courses, in the clinical setting, and also for the exam that looms immediately after graduation—the National Council Licensing Exam (NCLEX®). Passing the NCLEX-RN® is required before you are allowed to practice as a registered nurse.

So, nursing students must:

- Study for the long-term. The material you learned today you will have to know not only for the current course but also in other courses, on licensing exams and in your work setting.

- Have structured schedules. You must be willing to postpone ordinary pastimes, such as watching hours of television, in order to succeed in your academic work.

- Understand and retain more information than you ever have before.

Success = System + Schedule

The goal of this book is to provide academic support for aspiring nurses. Between them, the authors have over 35 years of working with students in the health sciences. They have developed a system of study that works. This system will help you retain the information presented in your classes and textbooks and will teach you to:

- Reduce stress by developing a manageable schedule
- Read efficiently
- Use critical thinking to organize essential information
- Create highly organized notes that are easy to review
- Recall and apply information for exams and clinical work

As a nursing student, you are making a big investment of your time and money in order to have a lifetime career as a registered nurse. If you follow our study system, you will be in a much better position to profit from your educational investment.

Studying for the Long Term

What Do We Know About Learning, Retention and Long-Term Memory?

Cramming for a test does not put information into long term memory. With a little bit of luck, you may recall enough from your "all-nighter" to squeeze by on the test the next day, but chances are that "crammed" information will be forgotten by the next week. Keeping a steady study schedule on a daily and weekly basis allows repeated reviews, which is what puts information into long-term memory.

In your ordinary life, what information do you have down pat? What telephone numbers, addresses, street routes, or facts do you easily remember? If you answer, "The ones I use over and over," you are absolutely correct. Psychologists who study learning and memory have shown repeatedly that going over and over information increases learning, memory, and long-term retention.

More than a century ago, a German experimental psychologist named Ebbinghaus described the process of forgetting. He called it the "Forgetting Curve." He also showed that you can slow down the forgetting process by periodically reviewing the information.

Ebbinghaus' Forgetting Curve

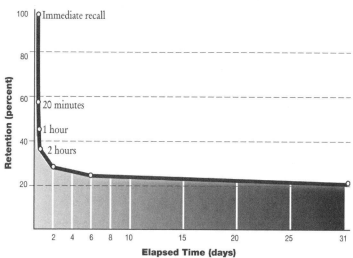

Figure 1.1

Tracking Study Habits For Exams

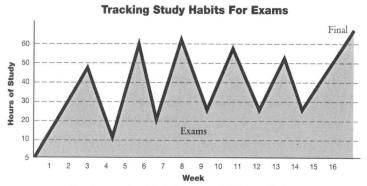

Figure 1.2   Frantic cramming right before tests and slacking off in between

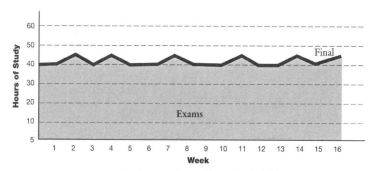

Figure 1.3   Keeping a regular weekly study schedule

How to Slow Down the Forgetting Process

The study system we teach in this book shows you how to slow down the process of forgetting by periodically reviewing the information you want to remember. For example, in our system you will have many opportunities to work with the information to be learned:

> **First**, you will preread rapidly before class;
> **Second** and **Third**, you will attend class and take notes;
> **Fourth** and **Fifth**, you will read the text and reorganize your notes into logical patterns that are easy to review and use for self-test;
> **Sixth** and **Seventh**, you will review your notes regularly (at least twice) between exams;
> **Eighth**, you will self-test at least once before exams.

We can hear you muttering, "Where will I find the time for all this review? I only review the material once now, and I hardly have enough time to do that!" The next chapter will show you where you can find time and how to plan a good study schedule. Remember, **Success = System + Schedule**. Devoting enough time to study is the foundation of a successful study system, which is why our book deals with time management first. After time-management, the chapters deal with each of the steps in the order listed above. We've added chapters on concentration (a great time-saver!), using productive self-talk, test-taking tips, and overcoming test anxiety.

The secret to success in almost anything is taking small steps that will lead you closer to your goal. In business this is often called a "kaizen" approach. We have broken each of the study skills in this book into small components that we think will be easy for you to apply. If a step seems too big to you, you can break it down further. The secret is to keep plugging away and taking small steps toward continual improvement.

Chapter Structure Patterned After the Nursing Process

This workbook is interactive. Each chapter follows a pattern similar to the **five-step nursing process** that is probably already familiar to you (or soon will be).

- **Assessment** is the first step. Thus, each chapter begins with a self-test. The self-assessment scoring guide reveals your own particular strengths and weaknesses related to the chapter topic.

- Each chapter also discusses the **goals** and **rationale** for adding this study skill to your regular practice. We provide background and references to show you why the content of each chapter is important in your overall study system.

- Next, one or more **interventions** are suggested. The interventions consist of exercises for immediate application to your current courses. You will be expected to put the study skill into practice for at least a week. Worksheets will be provided to record how you carried out these exercises.

- Finally, there is an **evaluation** or **follow-up**, during which you will reassess how the interventions affected your study strategies. What did you learn? How will you change your study habits in the future? You will be asked to think about and comment on what you learned from the chapter and from the recommended exercises.

The book is **student-centered** and requires **active partici-pation**. You will assess your own skill level on a number of components of a complete study system. Facts about these components are presented by the authors, usually in the Rationale section. You will then have the opportunity, through exercises in the Intervention section, to experience for yourself how these strategies affect your study skills. After the exercises, you will evaluate your own experience and decide which permanent changes in your study habits will lead to the greatest success—and decide if you are willing to make those changes.

This study skills system has been used successfully by medical students, veterinary medical students and other nursing students for many years. We hope the comments of some of our previous students at the end of each chapter under Student Feedback will motivate you toward shaping your own successful study system! If you ever find yourself slacking off, go back over the assessment and intervention sections on the skill you need to improve.

As with most professional training programs, the highest rate of attrition occurs in the first year of nursing school. You can avoid that scenario by implementing these methods immediately!

Who Will Benefit From This Book?

This book is for students who want to take charge of their own learning. If you are ready to make changes to your study strategies and are willing to follow our recommendations for at least the next six weeks, then let's get started!

Faculty at nursing schools where the students have been trained in our study system say they have observed improved class preparation, increased level of understanding and advanced critical thinking skills—all of which lead to higher grades!

> This study system works—if you work the system. That means using the worksheets and completing the exercises, not just reading the book.

Maintaining Motivation

Since your nursing school experience will be more like a marathon than a sprint, it is important to build in small rewards for yourself along the way in order to keep up your motivation. These rewards can be as small as having a snack, a verbal "pat on the back," listening to a favorite piece of music, taking a walk, or enjoying a hot bath. An evening getaway for a movie and dinner could be a larger reward. Plan these treats ahead of time and reward yourself when you've accomplished what you set out to do. Enjoy the fruits of your labor!

A secret to maintaining motivation is to learn to "reward the effort." Don't wait until the end of a semester or even when an exam comes around. Reward yourself for prereading every day. Reward yourself for creating a beautiful set of study notes. Reward yourself for putting in the number of study hours you needed this week.

The one thing to keep in mind about rewards is that your reward should not get you "off track" in your studies. Just as a dieter should not reward herself for losing ten pounds by eating an entire carton of ice cream, neither should a student reward herself for a good exam grade by missing the next few classes. Choose a reward that will keep you on track with your goals and that you can enjoy guilt-free!

Keep your rewards short and sweet and bestow them frequently!

How to Use This Book

It will take you about six weeks to work through the material in this book. Since the text is meant to be interactive, it will not be helpful to just read it without doing the assessments, exercises, and evaluations. The sequence of topics is carefully designed; therefore, we do not recommend skipping around the chapters.

Scheduling time is first, because you can't accomplish the rest of the system unless you have scheduled enough time. Prereading comes second, because it is the first step in the five-step system we recommend. You get the idea.

Week 1   Read and complete the exercises in Chapters 2 (Time) and 3 (Prereading).

Week 2   Read and complete the exercises in Chapter 4 (Structure the Content: Read and Make Notes) —and continue practicing time management and prereading.

Week 3   Read and complete the exercises in Chapter 5 (Encode the Information: Review and Self-Test). Add this strategy to time management, prereading, reading and note making. This is the last element of our study system. The rest of the book consists of advice on how to improve your ability to use the system.

Week 4   Read and complete the exercises in Chapter 6 (Keeping Focused).

Week 5   Read and complete the exercises in Chapter 7 (Productive Self Talk).

Week 6 Chapters 8 and 9 have information on preparing for classroom exams and the NCLEX. (Even though the NCLEX seems far in the future, you will be glad you read Chapter 9 as you start nursing school, because you will keep better records and notes!)

Some of the worksheets in this book are available on our website, www.vitalstudyskills.com, if you would like a full-sized version.

Current Study Strategies

Take a few minutes and briefly describe your current study strategies in the space below. How do you prepare for classes and/or exams?

_____

_____

_____

_____

_____

_____

After you complete this workbook, we'll ask you to return to this section so you can discover the changes you have made in how you approach your studies.

Student Feedback

The following comments are from nursing students who have used this study system.

This method of studying helped me bring my grades up. I now study more efficiently and effectively. After I finish studying, I feel confident.

It helps me keep my time straight, and I've found the study strategies that work for me. I know what to study at a particular time, and I review my notes at least three times before the test.

Before learning this study system, I didn't really have any study strategy. After learning this study system, I have my time planned out, I preread, take notes and self-test. These strategies are really helping me to study better and know the material well.

The information will stay with me forever—even after nursing school. This is really, really helpful for everyone.

As far as I'm concerned, this study system works.

My study habits have changed greatly. I now realize I can accomplish a lot by using my time wisely—concentrating on the task at hand and reading in a much smarter and faster fashion.

For me, this was a new way of looking at the material. It helped me to see different views and incorporate them into my own strategy.

 References
(Just So You'll Know We Didn't Make This Up!)

All Nursing Schools. (2006). *Types of nursing programs.* Retrieved December 7, 2006, from http://www.allnursingschools.com

> This website has a wealth of information concerning nursing, including the various types of nursing programs.

Bureau of Labor Statistics, U.S. Department of Labor. (2006-2007).
Occupational outlook handbook, 2006-07 edition, Registered
Nurses. Retrieved December 7, 2006, from http://www.bls.gov/
oco/ ocos083.htm

> Standard reference giving basic information on most work
> classifications, including working conditions, salaries and outlook
> for future employment.

Boring, E.G., Langfeld, H.S., and Weld, H.P. (1948). *Foundations of
psychology*. New York: John Wiley.

> Chapter 8 addresses the issue of how information is retained.

Clark, R., Nguyen, F., & Sweller, J. (2006). *Efficiency in learning: Evidence-
based guidelines to manage cognitive load*. San Francisco: Pfeiffer.

> The guidelines in this book are based on more than 25 years of
> research conducted by John Sweller and his associates. Application
> of the cognitive load theory leads to efficient learning by minimiz-
> ing or eliminating irrelevant material and emphasizing that which
> is relevant.

Ebbinghaus, H. (1885). *Uber das gedachnis*. Leipzig, Germany: Dunker &
Humbolt.

> Ebbinghaus was one of the first scientists to study learning and
> forgetting. His work has withstood the test of time and is still often
> quoted.

Eliot, J. (2004). *Overachievement: The new model for exceptional performance*.
New York: Portfolio.

> The author has done field work observing and interviewing high
> performers and now advises clients on how to use stress to their
> advantage to perform at the highest level possible.

Farr, M.J. (1987). *The long-term retention of knowledge and skills*. New York:
Springer-Verlag.

> A literature review of memory, learning and retention. Refers to
> work published by Ebbinghaus in 1885.

Foshay, W.R., Silber, K.H., & Stelnicki, M.B. (2003). *Writing training
materials that work*. San Francisco: Jossey-Bass/Pfeiffer.

> A guide based on current cognitive psychology and instructional
> design theory and research. This book addresses creating instruc-

tional materials, which is the same task that students must undertake when they make their own study notes.

Gerson, R.F., & Gerson, R.G. (2006, June). Effort management. *Training + Development*, American Society for Training and Development, pp. 26-27.

Research in attribution theory and motivation indicates that rewarding both effort and achievement induces people to be more willing to do a task again and even take on more difficult challenges.

Health Resources and Services Administration, Bureau of Health Professions. (2002). *Projected supply, demand, and shortages of registered nurses: 2002-2020*. Washington, D.C.: U.S. Department of Health and Human Services.

The title says it all.

Maurer, R. (2004). *One small step can change your life: The kaizen way*. New York: Workman Publishing.

Maurer suggests the following actions to bring about change: ask small questions, think small thoughts, take small actions, bestow small rewards, identify small moments.

Potolsky, A., Cohen, J., & Saylor, C. (2003). Academic performance of nursing students: Do prerequisite grades and tutoring make a difference? *Nursing Education Perspective*, Volume 24, 5, 246-250.

"Most attrition occurs in the first year of the program. Hence it is best to offer retention programs in the first semester."

Spitzer, H.F. (1939). Studies in retention. *Journal of Educational Psychology*, 30, 641-656.

Concludes that review of notes should comprise most of a student's study time.

Scheduling Your Time for Success

(Weeks 1 and 2)

> *Even though my weeks in nursing school are demanding, there really is time for everything—it's just a matter of time management.*

✓ Assessment: Time Usage

| Never | Rarely | Sometimes | Often | Always |

Directions: Circle the number that best describes how you use your time during the school term.

0 1 2 3 4   1. Appointments and important tasks are recorded in my personal calendar.

4 3 2 1 0   2. I take a break from studying for a couple of days right after an exam.

4 3 2 1 0   3. There is no time to sleep just before tests.

0 1 2 3 4   4. During an hour of study, I take no more than a 10-minute break.

4 3 2 1 0   5. I find myself running late for classes, appointments or other activities.

0 1 2 3 4   6. I get 7-8 hours of sleep most nights.

Never	Rarely	Sometimes	Often	Always		

4 3 2 1 0   7.   Friends' calls or visits often interrupt my study plans.

0 1 2 3 4   8.   I decline invitations or involvement in projects that might sabotage my study schedule.

0 1 2 3 4   9.   I carry study materials with me so I can use small bits of time that might other wise be wasted, like waiting for class to begin, between classes, or waiting for a friend.

4 3 2 1 0   10. I wait until I'm "in the mood" to begin studying.

4 3 2 1 0   11. I do most of my studying on the weekends.

4 3 2 1 0   12. I watch television more than two hours per day.

0 1 2 3 4   13. I spend close to two hours in personal study for every hour of lecture I attend.

4 3 2 1 0   14. I spend more than one hour a day in personal care (e.g., grooming and hygiene).

0 1 2 3 4   15. I exercise two or three times a week.

_____   **Total Score** *(sum of circled numbers)*

Mark "yes" or "no" in response to the following questions.

___Yes ___No   16. I work (paid employment) twelve or
more hours per week.

___Yes ___No   17. I commute one or more hour(s) per day.

___Yes ___No   18. My parental or familial responsibili-
ties take at least four hours per day.

Feedback on Time Usage Answers

1. Why waste mental energy trying to remember all
   the details of your daily schedule instead of
   writing them down? It's much easier and less
   stressful to write down what you need to do and
   then check it off when it's done. **Of course you'll
   have to check your schedule every day—that's
   the whole point!**

2. Go back to the Introduction (Chapter 1) and
   have a look at the two figures comparing the
   "steady rate" of study with the cramming. With a
   steady study schedule you can eliminate the stress
   and fear that come with falling behind. **The take
   home message is—get right back on your study
   schedule after an exam!**

3. Here's where keeping a schedule pays off! If you
   have kept to your study schedule, then you can be
   rested and relaxed (okay, relatively relaxed) before
   an exam while your friends are panicking.

4. Study during your scheduled study time. A break
   of no more than 10 minutes is okay, but don't

allow yourself to overextend your break. Never count an hour as an hour of study unless you actually study at least **50 minutes** of it.

5. **Being on time** is the sign of a well-managed schedule. If you are running late, you may be over-scheduling, not being realistic in making time estimates, or not consulting your schedule on a regular basis. Faculty members asked us to emphasize to students that being on time is a professional behavior that is expected of nursing students and can even affect their grades.

6. If you answered "always" or "often," good for you! Not getting enough sleep is actually a waste of time, because you are not fully awake and alert in class or while you are studying. Besides, according to recent research, not getting enough sleep can lead to a depressed immune system and even to overeating.

7. It's hard to put friends off, but these situations give you the opportunity to practice setting boundaries. You can save your schedule by setting a date to meet that person at another time to spend some time together. **If you let other people encroach on your time, you may come to resent them, so don't get started down that road.** Nip it in the bud!

8. It's more awkward to have to cancel an invitation you accepted without checking your schedule than it is to politely decline an invitation in the first place. **If you're not sure what you've scheduled, say, "It sounds like fun. Let me check my schedule, and I'll get back to you."**

9. Always carry something convenient to study. Chapter 4 (on note-making) offers suggestions about what notes are convenient to carry with you. Using little bits of time frees up other time. Brief reviews are a gift of time!

10. As a nurse, you will not have the luxury of going to work only when you "feel like it"—so do yourself the favor of learning how to be in a good mood while you do what you have to do anyway. (Chapter 7 on self-talk can help you with this.) An added benefit of using productive self-talk: The intent to remember will actually help you retain the information you are studying.

11. There is not enough time on the weekends to do all your studying if you are a full-time student. A good rule of thumb is to plan to study one to two hours for every hour of lecture, depending on how many credit hours you are taking. You won't be able to fit all that studying into a weekend. Also, if an unexpected event comes up, you have no leeway if you have planned a massive weekend study session. Realistically, how much will you retain from two fifteen-hour marathon study sessions?

12. Everybody needs a break now and then, but wouldn't you be happier and more satisfied with your life if you spent the time achieving your goal instead of watching reruns? If you could have back all your wasted hours, you'd have a whole new life.

13. Good! You should.

14. Gone are the days when you could spend hours in

personal grooming; you're in nursing school now and don't have the free time.

15. Health care professionals need a healthy lifestyle. Use physical exercise as part of your recreation. You can even combine social life with exercise by walking or playing tennis with a friend.

16. The hard truth is that it's very difficult to work while attending nursing school full time. A full-time job usually will not leave enough time for studying. If you are working more than 12-16 hours per week, it's time to reconsider your goals and values. Some programs even advise their students to keep their work load below 10 hours per week. If you must work more, you might need to look for a nursing program that permits a more flexible schedule and take a little more time to get your degree. Talk with your nursing school advisor about options for a more flexible schedule. Some programs will allow you to extend the time it takes to complete the program.

    A part-time program would allow you to work towards your goal of being an RN while continuing to meet the needs of those who are financially dependent on you. Life is full of trade-offs, but that does NOT mean you have to give up your goal—it just may take you a bit longer. If your situation includes supporting a family, you are simply not in the same situation as a single person with no responsibilities other than school.

17. If you spend much time commuting, make travel-time study-time! You can listen to recordings of lectures or recordings you have made yourself,

Vital Skills

reading from your own notes. If you share a ride with a fellow student you have a built-in study partner! (Chapter 4 shows you how to make easily reviewable notes.) That said, you must still keep your eyes and attention on the road! You may need to turn off the tape and the talk when the traffic demands your full attention.

18. Students with family responsibilities have a special challenge. Families require time and attention. Here again, as in item # 16 above, you must weigh the merits of being a part-time student vs. a full-time student. Some students find that, realistically, they may need to extend their period of study in order to accomplish both goals of raising a family and becoming an RN.

Score Interpretation — Time Usage

If your Total Score on the first 15 items is in the **45-60** range, you don't need to spend much time on this chapter. You're a very good time manager. See if you can pick up a few tips in the rest of the chapter.

If your score is in the **30-44** range, you have an idea of what you should be doing but need to improve. The exercises in this chapter will help you better manage your time.

If your score was **below 30**, time management may be the key to your success. Remember:

Success = System + **Schedule**

You need a better schedule before you can implement the system.

Goal: Create a Workable Schedule

The goal is to create a schedule that allows one to two hours of study for every hour of lecture. This study system has been extremely successful for the students who adopt it, but you must allocate adequate time.

 # Rationale

If you are not putting in enough hours of study, all the study techniques in the world will be useless. You must dedicate the time required to learn the material. Given that basic fact, what will your schedule look like?

As we mentioned earlier, full-time nursing students are typically scheduled for about fifteen credits per semester. The usual expectation at this level of education is that one semester credit requires about two hours of personal study time. Thus, a full-time student can expect to spend 40-45 hours each week studying, counting both scheduled class time and personal study time.

What About Online Courses?

The same principles that apply to succeeding in the traditional classroom also apply to doing well in online courses. In fact, the time planning and management element becomes even more vital because less structure is imposed on your time. Even if you won't be sitting in a traditional classroom for your courses, the strategies in this book will still help you achieve your academic goals.

Where Can Students Find the Time?

Students often say, "There isn't enough time to do everything I need to do!"

About half of the students who begin our study skills course report that they spend ten hours or less per week in personal study, which is, frankly, not enough to succeed. Many students are married or have a significant companion who expects to receive some time and attention. Others are parents (sometimes single parents) who are working part time.

Faculty members state that many of their nursing students do not, for varied reasons, dedicate enough time to their studies and are, therefore, not prepared for either their classes or their exams. Realistically, is there enough time to combine full-time study with students' other responsibilities?

Let's do the calculation:

Available *hours per week*	168 hours
Average time spent per week in class	15 hours
Number of hours suggested for personal study per week	30 hours
Clinical work and Care Plans	14 hours
Sleep (average of 7 hours per night)	49 hours
Everything else!	60 hours

If that sounds like plenty of time for exercising, relaxing, having fun with friends and family, eating, personal hygiene, etc., here are some additional facts to throw into the calculation:

> Many nursing students commute between 1-2 hours per day, leaving only 54 hours for everything else. Also, some students work between 12-24 hours a week. If we subtract 18 hours (the middle of the work hours range), then you have only 36 hours left each week for "living."

How much time should we subtract for time and attention to a spouse or significant other? How much time should be subtracted for care of and attention to children? We haven't even begun to account for time to buy, prepare and eat food. How about personal hygiene? Exercise? Cleaning house and doing laundry?

Is it any wonder that many students initially report only a few hours of personal study per week? If you follow our prescriptions for time management in this chapter, you will "find" time you would otherwise "lose."

 Interventions: Part I

Exercise 1 — Estimate: How Do You Think You Use Your Time?

1. How much time do you spend in rest & recreation? (movies, TV, dancing, sports, reading or other pleasurable activities)

    _____ hours per day _____ hours per week

2. How many hours do you spend in lectures and clinical work?

    _____ hours per day _____ hours per week

3. How many hours do you spend in personal study?
   _____ hours per day _____ hours per week

4. How many hours do you spend in study groups?
   _____ hours per day _____ hours per week

5. How many hours do you spend in maintenance activities? (housework, chores, shopping, etc.)
   _____ hours per day _____hours per week

6. How many hours do you sleep on average per night?
   _____ hours per night during the week
   _____ hours per night on weekends

Now let's do a reality check. For the next week, we'd like for you to keep track of where your time really goes. Follow the directions in Exercise 2 below.

Exercise 2 — The Reality: How Do You Really Use Your Time?

Most people do not have an accurate count of their time usage. The only way to find out is to keep track of it. Use the following form to record your activities for the next week. Tally the numbers by category to see how you are allocating your time. By being totally honest in completing this exercise, you will probably discover wasted bits (or huge chunks) of time that can be converted into more productive activities. You may even find some "play time" that you didn't realize you had!

Carry a Time Recording Sheet (page 32) with you for the next week. You may want to fill in all your scheduled activities first (classes, regular meetings, work, commute, worship services, any appointments to which you are already committed). If you need more room to write, a larger version of the Time Recording Sheet is available on our website: www.vitalstudyskills.com.

Record your activities in one hour units using the categories below:

- Lecture (LEC)

- Clinical (CLN)

- Personal Study (PS) — but don't count it as an hour of study unless you spent at least 50 minutes of the hour in actual study time.

- Maintenance (M) This includes chores such as housecleaning, car care, laundry, shopping for necessities, etc. *Note:* Any shopping that is "fun" is R&R.)

- Paid Employment (Job)

- Commute (COM)

- Physical Exercise (PE)

- It may not seem fair, but count everything else as rest and recreation (R&R).

- Sleep (S)

When calculating Personal Study (PS) time, don't count it as an hour of study unless you spent at least 50 minutes of the hour in actual study time. We can't emphasize this point too much. As one of our nursing students discovered, "I end up taking a break from studying and don't go back to it until hours later."

Begin Chapter 3 — Prereading

While you are recording your time this week, read and do the exercises in Chapter Three, Prereading. Prereading is an invaluable time-saver. Adding this new study skill will make lectures more interesting, speed up your reading of the text, increase your comprehension and give you a jump-start on making a good set of study notes.

Go to Chapter 3 on Prereading. Meanwhile…

 ## Evaluation: Part I

Check-Up for Exercise 2 — Time Recording

Answer the questions below after recording your time for one week.

    1. What did you learn about how you use your time?

_____

_____

_____

_____

_____

_____

_____

2. How many hours did you spend in your total academic activities (attending classes or clinical work, personal study time, etc?) How does your total compare with the recommended 40-45 hours per week average for a full-time student? (Or two hours for every credit hour for part-time students.)

_____

_____

_____

_____

_____

Look at your completed Baseline Time Recording Sheet to answer these questions:

3. How much R&R time did you tally?
_____ hours per week

4. What was your total time in attendance for lectures and clinical? _____ hours per week

6. What was the total number of hours of personal study time? _____ hours per week

7. Maintenance activities took how much time this past week? _____ hours per week

8. What was your sleep average per night?
_____ hours per weeknight
_____ hours per night on weekends

9. Now compare these figures to your estimates in Exercise 1. Were your original estimates close to how much time you actually spend on these activities?

_____

_____

_____

_____

_____

_____

10. Are there changes you would like to make based on what you have learned thus far? If so, list one or two of the more important changes.

_____

_____

_____

_____

_____

_____

Baseline Time Recording Sheet

Record your activities in ½ hour or 1 hour blocks for a week. At the end of the week calculate the totals for the major activities using the following categories: Lecture, Clinical, PS (personal study), M (maintenance activities including shopping, meal preparation, cleaning, errands, eating, etc.), Job, COM (commute time), PE (physical exercise), R&R (rest and recreation, including anything that does not fit into the other categories) and S (sleep).

	Mon	Tues	Wed	Thurs	Fri	Sat	Sun
5:00 a.m.							
5:30							
6:00							
6:30							
7:00							
7:30							
8:00							
9:00							
10:00							
11:00							
11:30							
12:00							
12:30							
1:00 p.m.							
2:00							
3:00							
4:00							
5:00							
6:00							
6:30							
7:00							
7:30							
8:00							
8:30							
9:00							
9:30							
10:00							
10:30							
11:00							
11:30							
12:00							
1:00 a.m.							
2:00 a.m.							
Daily: LEC							
CLN							
PS							
COM							
Job							
Maint.							
PE							
R&R							
Sleep							

Actual weekly totals: Lecture = _____ Clinical = _____ Personal Study = _____ Commute = _____

Job = _____ Maintenance = _____ Physical Exercise = _____ R&R = _____ Sleep = _____

Worksheet 2.1

Vital Skills

Student Feedback, Part I

After tracking their time and then developing an individualized schedule, here are some of the students' comments.

Keeping a schedule helps me keep my time straight. I know what to study at a particular time, and I now have time to review my notes several times before the test!

I need to have a schedule of what I am to do with myself at all times and follow it.

Keeping a schedule forces me to manage my time better.

I am learning to be more time conscious now and try to make my time count for something.

Take Charge of Your Own Schedule

Planning Study Time

Now that you have a better idea of how you actually spend your time, you are ready to make some important decisions about planning a good schedule. Block out times for personal study when you can concentrate for at least an hour. Two hours would be even better. You should have at least one such concentrated study session every day. Schedule this block of time when you can be reasonably certain not to be interrupted. If you think two hours at a stretch is too long to maintain your concentration, at least aim for it. Sitting still and focusing your attention is a learned skill. It is called endurance. By making a plan to study for two consecutive hours, you may be able to extend your period of concentration. (See Chapter 6 for ideas to help you increase your concentration and endurance.)

Taking a ten or fifteen minute break for refreshment or vigorous exercise in the middle of this study session will help you extend your period of concentrated study. And remember that a concentrated study period does not have to mean all that time is spent on one topic or activity. It just means that the time is dedicated to studying—be it prereading, reading, note making or reviewing—and nothing else. Maintenance activities and R&R should be planned for time when you feel less mentally energetic or need a break from an intense period of study.

Try to schedule a study period immediately after lecture, when possible. The ideas from the lecture are fresh in your mind. It will be easier to consolidate your notes and compare information from the lecture with the syllabus, textbook or handouts over the same topic.

Now that you've begun prereading, go ahead and schedule ten to fifteen minutes of prereading before each lecture. If your lectures are in a long block, try to preread immediately before the block. Prereading saves time by getting you a better set of notes during the lecture.

Scheduling Study Periods

In later chapters we will discuss study activities that take only a few minutes at a time. While reviewing, for instance, brief but frequent sessions are a much more effective use of time than marathon sessions. Initially, creation of your highly-organized, condensed notes will require a major investment of time. If two hours is simply not a possibility, then start with one-hour periods and build up from there.

When to schedule your study time is an individual decision, but many students tell us that mornings and afternoons work better than waiting until closer to bedtime. You might choose to get up before anyone else at home or stay on campus until early evening to complete your studies. Weekends should also be part of your regular study routine. Most students find they must dedicate at least four to six hours to studying on weekends.

Exercise and Study Breaks

Aim for thirty minutes of exercise every day. That long walk to and from your car counts!

In addition to regular physical exercise, it's important to give yourself short "refreshing breaks" during long study sessions. For example, playing the piano, listening (or dancing) to a favorite piece of music, taking a short walk, enjoying a period of meditation or inspirational reading are all useful rewards for a good study session. Even putting a load of laundry in to wash will get you up and moving around. Bet you never thought of doing laundry as a "break"!

Another idea for a break is to step outside and be mindful of the day, the weather, the sky, trees, birds, all the life around you. It can be quite energizing. These activities can disengage your busy thoughts from a myriad of details, allow you to think about the bigger picture of your life and even motivate you to study for longer periods of time.

Managing Your Schedule

Managing your time is a habit. Behavioral scientists tell us that the best way to develop and control habits is to use continual feedback until your new habits become established routines. So continue to keep track of your time, as you move on to the next set of worksheets.

You may need to tweak your plans as you go along. You can't tell your brother that his emergency surgery doesn't fit into your schedule! When the unplanned happens, the lost study time needs to be made up. This make-up time will likely come from previously scheduled R&R or maintenance activities.

We suggest that you only "swap time" within the same week. Why? With your tight schedule, you won't have the time to borrow from next week. That's the slippery slope that leads to cramming, losing sleep, and falling back into old, unproductive study patterns.

If you often find yourself having to "borrow" or "swap" time, take another look at your schedule. Are you unrealistic in estimating how long things take? Do you allow unplanned activities to interfere? Find out what needs to be changed and change it!

Plan Enough Time for Sleep

In the last few years, research has been conducted on the physiological effects of lack of sleep. Not surprisingly, the research shows that sleep loss impairs learning and memory. Sleep research conducted at the University of Chicago has shown that four hours sleep per night for six consecutive nights, hormone function is impaired and a number of bodily functions are degraded. Cortisol levels rise, the body isn't able to regulate insulin levels. Some of the results are impaired cognitive function and the likelihood of weight gain. The young men who volunteered for the sleep-loss study began with blood tests in the normal range and at the end of the one-week study had blood test results similar to those of diabetics! The good news is that after resuming healthy sleep patterns for several nights their blood tests were once again in the normal range.

Even though individuals vary in how much sleep is enough, the amount needed by adults to function at optimal levels is typically between seven and nine hours per night. Yes, naps can help you reclaim some lost night time sleep, but naps need to be kept to less than two hours and you need to be back up again by 5 p.m. or your night time sleep may be affected.

Scientists at the University of California-San Francisco,

also have evidence that studying until you are tired and then "sleeping on it" improves next day exam performance more than "pulling an all-nighter." Improved nerve cell connections during sleep seems to be the reason for this finding.

"Pulling an all-nighter."

Schedule Time for Friends and Family

Save some time for the special people in your life and schedule it in. Write it down on your schedule as R&R. Time spent with those we care about is one of life's greatest joys and an investment in future happiness. Since we all have to eat, meals are a wonderful time to reconnect with family and friends!

Now, let's *plan* a weekly schedule!

 Intervention: Part II

Exercise 3 — Plan Your Schedule for the Next Week (Plan/Actual)

Use the Plan/Actual Time Recording Sheet on page 41 to

plan your schedule for the next week. Make as many copies as you need before you write on it. Now schedule in the "Plan" column all your high priority activities, such as lecture, clinical or small group meetings. Also schedule other necessary activities: job, physical exercise, meals, sleep and R&R. Mark on the "Plan" side when you want to do your personal study. Carry this schedule with you every day.

You will need to refer to it during the day to be sure you are following your plan. You'll feel positively noble as you check off completion of your plan each hour in the "Actual" column. If you did not follow your plan, make a note in the "Actual" column of what you really did with that unit of time.

While you are monitoring your time this second week, move on to Chapter 4, Read and Make Notes. Don't go past Chapter 4. Take time to digest all the information on note-making. It is the heart of the Vital Skills Study System.

At the end of the Plan/Actual Time Recording week, return to this chapter and complete "Check-up for Exercise 3—Plan/Actual Time Recording".

Read Chapter 4, Read and Make Notes

 ## Evaluation: Part II

Check-up for Exercise 3 — Plan/Actual Time Recording

Briefly write your answers to the following questions, based on what you have learned from monitoring your time for the past week, using the Plan/Actual Time Recording Sheet.

1. How close did you come to completing your plan?

_____

_____

_____

_____

_____

2. If you weren't close, why not? What did you substitute for planned activities? Can you detect a pattern? For example, did spending too much time in R & R cut down on study time?

_____

_____

_____

_____

_____

3. What changes are necessary?

_____

_____

_____

_____

_____

4. If you had to choose just one helpful idea you learned from this chapter on scheduling your time, what would it be?

_____

_____

_____

_____

_____

_____

_____

If you kept reasonably close to your planned schedule— *Congratulations!* You can now switch to a regular appointment book or PDA (personal digital assistant) for scheduling activities. Buy one that fits easily into your backpack, or whatever you carry around with you all day, but is large enough to record all your activities.

If your actual time spent was NOT close to what you had planned, you will benefit from another week of completing a Plan/Actual Time Recording Sheet. Revise your plan for the next week, using this experience and analysis, and do a second week of Plan/Actual Time Recording.

It's interesting (and rewarding!) to think about how to accomplish your goals with maximum efficiency. You may have developed some slick tricks of your own to save time. Here are some time-saving tips gleaned from busy students who manage to remember friends and family, do all the things they have to do, keep clean and fed and still spend 40-50 hours each week in learning activities.

Plan / Actual Time Recording Sheet

Plan your activities for one week. Put a check beside the items you complete at the scheduled time. Write in what you actually did if it was different from your plan. At the end of the week calculate the totals for the major activities using the following categories: Lecture, Clinical, PS (personal study), M (maintenance activities including shopping, meal preparation, cleaning, errands, eating, etc.), Job, COM (commute time), PE (physical exercise), R&R (rest and recreation, including anything that does not fit into the other categories) and S (sleep).

	Mon		Tues		Wed		Thurs		Fri		Sat		Sun	
	plan	actual	plan	actual	plan	actual	plan	actual	plan	actual	plan	actual	plan	actual
5:00 a.m.														
5:30														
6:00														
6:30														
7:00														
7:30														
8:00														
9:00														
10:00														
11:00														
11:30														
12:00														
12:30														
1:00 p.m.														
2:00														
3:00														
4:00														
5:00														
6:00														
6:30														
7:00														
7:30														
8:00														
8:30														
9:00														
9:30														
10:00														
10:30														
11:00														
11:30														
12:00														
1:00 a.m.														
2:00 a.m.														
Daily: LEC														
CLN														
PS														
COM														
Job														
Maint.														
PE														
R&R														
Sleep														

Actual weekly totals: Lecture = _____ Clinical = _____ Personal Study = _____ Commute = _____
Job = _____ Maintenance = _____ Physical Exercise = _____ R&R = _____ Sleep = _____

Worksheet 2.2

Things You Can Do to Save Time

1. Do two maintenance or R&R activities at the same time. (Note that these are activities that do not typically require a great deal of focused concentration.)

   • Listen to music or catch the news or your favorite TV program while performing maintenance tasks, such as preparing meals, fixing your hair or shaving.

   • Exercise while watching TV or a DVD.

   • Sort through your note cards or other notes (See Chapter 5) while waiting for something/ someone.

   • Many social activities can be combined with exercise. Walk, jog or go to the gym with a friend. You can keep in touch and fight flab at the same time.

   • Share a meal with a friend. When a friend's call interrupts your study, you can say, "I'm in the middle of something right now, but I'd love to see you. How about lunch tomorrow?"

2. Many of the "things I have to do" can be accomplished in less time, if you are willing to change your style.

   • Get a haircut that you can fix in five or ten minutes (really!).

- Eat food that requires little preparation. "Fast" food needn't be unhealthy. Fresh vegetables and fruits, served with cheese, come to mind. Dropping a few nuts in a container of yogurt can be a small meal or a snack. You get the idea.

3. Keep lists for all your regular activities:

   - To avoid extra trips to the store, put items on a "To Buy" list as soon as the need arises. Never go shopping without your list. Bonus: You'll not only save time, you'll also save money if you stick to your list.

   - Keep a "To Do" errand list and combine as many trips as are practical. Schedule errands on an efficient route to minimize time and mileage. For example, find the most efficient route for the grocery store, service station, hardware store, or wherever and try not to go out on just one errand at a time. Aim to complete at least three errands per trip to save both time and gas.

4. Always carry your schedule book or PDA with you.

5. "Post-it™" notes are great for sticking on a page for temporary reminders and are easily removed as the task is completed.

6. "Pending" files are great for items you want to save or remember for the short term. Coupons (two dinners for the price of one), tickets, etc., can go in the "pending" file for retrieval as needed.

Go through your pending file regularly, maybe once a

month, and remove anything that has expired and can no longer be used. This is the one case where procrastination can pay! And it keeps your desk space uncluttered.

7. A " bills" file for all those statements that come in the mail that you don't have time to deal with immediately. Go through this file every week or two. Bills unpaid past the deadline often cost you extra time, money and headaches. Just putting them away in a file helps keep your desk clear of clutter. To cut down on the number of bills you have to physically deal with each month, consider automatic payments from your bank or credit union checking account (also saves money on stamps).

8. Be a person who remembers others, even if you are extremely busy. Mark birthdays and other special occasions on your calendar (ahead of the date, so you can send a card or gift on time). Some students carry a PDA, which makes it even easier. At the same moment you see it's your sister's birthday, you can call and wish her happiness on her special day.

9. Do you wander around your home muttering, "Where did I put my… (fill in the blank)?" You can avoid this annoying time-waster by having a regular, assigned place for everything. This applies especially to small articles that you constantly pick up and put down again, such as keys, glasses, watches, wallets or purses.

10. Try to do things when other people don't. Go to an early movie and eat afterwards. Avoid grocery shopping between 5 p.m. and 6 p.m., or whenever your store is likely to be crowded.

11. Use care in your consumption of alcohol. That extra drink or two the night before can lead to "blowing" much of the next day. It's hard to pay attention to lectures or studying if you have a headache.

12. Protect study time. If a friend begins talking with you while studying, tell him you'd like to have a good visit, pull out your calendar and find convenient time to get together. Or, say you plan to take a short break at a specific time and would enjoy a chat then.

When the telephone interrupts your study time at home, you have options:

- Don't answer. If you have an answering machine, the caller can leave a message, and you can call back later when it's more convenient. This system also screens out unwanted calls.

- If you can't stand not answering the phone when it rings, turn off the ringer or unplug it during study periods.

Some students pre-empt interruptions by making phone calls between classes, so their social or familial obligations will be taken care of before they begin a study period.

13. Do you study at home with family nearby? Work out a signal that lets family members know when you are studying and don't want to be disturbed unless the house is on fire.

- One student said she shuts the door and puts up a "Do Not Disturb" sign.

- Many students tell us that early mornings, before other family members awake, are often a good time to study.

- Those with older children sometimes find that they are able to sit with their children at a large table while they all work on their studies together.

- Other students find that staying on campus for all their study activities works best for them.

14. Study groups with friends can be a bonus, or they can be a problem. Study groups are a problem if the time is regularly spent socializing rather than studying. The "50-minute rule" can help you decide if a study group is how you want to spend your valuable study time. Study group time counts as R&R if more than 10 minutes of any hour is spent off topic. If the group's time is often taken up with complaining about a particular instructor, talking about relationships, or lack thereof, etc., then you may want to arrange to meet this group of friends for lunch or a coffee break and spend your precious study time focused on the subject you need to study.

Students who belong to effective study groups, tell us that the participants have agreed to spend time outside the group studying and learning the material and then come together to review and test each other on it. These groups can also be helpful for those who sometimes get "stuck" while making their study notes. You can get together to share ideas about the approach you've taken to a particular topic.

15. A digital timer is a great study tool. Using a timer

can help you keep track of both study periods and break times. It's a good way to figure out how long things actually take and can also help keep you on task. They are inexpensive and useful in many situations.

Benefits of Procrastination

You probably never expected to see a section on the benefits of procrastination in a book about study skills. But let's face it; if there were no benefits to procrastination then no one would do it. People who are life-long procrastinators tell us:

- Procrastination gives you a "rush" when you are able to complete the project just minutes (or seconds) ahead of the deadline.

- Procrastination gives you a built-in excuse for failure. "Oh, I put it off too long. If I had started earlier I would have succeeded."

- Procrastinators feel they are "getting away with" something by waiting until the last possible moment to begin a project.

But, as you can well imagine, there are also downsides to procrastination.

- Procrastination does not allow you to do your best work. There is no time for reflection or fine-tuning.

- Procrastination creates anxiety, which may cause you to avoid the task at hand. (Which in turn creates more stress and anxiety as you fall further behind!)

- Procrastination sets up a cycle of wasting time and then trying to reclaim that time all at once.

- Procrastination does not allow for the inevitable reality of delays, mistakes and illnesses that occur in everyone's life.

If you examine the two lists above, you will notice that the first list (the perceived "benefits" of procrastination) involves transitory emotions. Achieving excellence is not part of the procrastination pay-off. If you are a chronic postponer, you know there are other feelings that also go along with procrastinating, such as guilt, fear, dread, worry, anxiety and sometimes anger. Procrastination is like gambling with time: You get an initial rush from the risk, but the long-term effect is harmful. Odds are, sooner or later, some unexpected event will derail you.

The good news is that behavioral experts believe that procrastination is just a bad habit and can be remedied like any other habit you would like to replace. First, by becoming aware of the habit or pattern and then, by taking the steps necessary to remedy it. Once you begin to reap the rewards of having a steady study schedule, you won't want to return to the anxiety-ridden days of procrastinating!

For those who offer the excuse that they "do their best work under pressure," we suggest that you can create your own "pressure" which will not have nearly the disastrous consequences of missing a deadline. For example, if the teacher says your 20-page paper on "Health Benefits of Regular Hand Washing" is due on a Monday morning, you could set your deadline to finish the paper on the Friday evening prior to that date. If you mark it in your calendar and tell yourself it MUST be finished by that date, then you can still enjoy the thrill of working under pressure, while also building in a day or two to review and improve your paper. If you take the time to review and revise your work, you are also likely to receive a higher grade, which should also help reinforce your new habit of setting an early deadline.

A final consideration regarding procrastination would be to re-examine your study area. Is it messy, cluttered or uninviting in some way? If so, this could be one of the reasons you don't like to use that space. Look at Chapter 6, Keeping Focused, for some ideas on how to arrange your study area so you can get the maximum benefit from your study time. You'll be amazed at how a properly equipped study space can boost your efficiency!

"Scheduling will keep you on track. Remember:
Success = System + Schedule!"

Exercise 4 — What Have You Learned?

1. What was the main thing you learned from working your way through this chapter on time management?

   _____

   _____

   _____

   _____

2. What is the single most important thing you need to change to become a better time manager?

   _____

   _____

   _____

   _____

 ## Summary

Some students of nursing find themselves in the challenging position of having to juggle school, family and employment. There will be a time of adjustment as you learn to prioritize and set boundaries. The more quickly you learn to do that—to figure out what needs to be done and then act on it—the shorter your period of adjustment will be.

If you are a person whose full time job is being a student—then you can consider yourself fortunate. By applying this study system you are in a good position to ace nursing school!

The exercises in this chapter have been designed to help you clearly understand how you spend your time and to plan a schedule that will help you achieve your goals as a nursing student. It takes time to get where you want to go. You can develop a good study system only if you schedule enough time for the job.

A bonus for excellent time scheduling is the feeling of confidence in knowing that you have designed your life to have enough time for all your responsibilities and your pleasures!

 ## Student Feedback, Part II

Spending a little time here and there doing nothing adds up to a big block of wasted time!

I waste a lot of time that could be used for studying.

Even though my week was demanding, there really is time for everything—it's just a matter of time management.

Study time allotted is plenty—I'm just not using it wisely. I realized I must schedule in some physical exercise.

It is important to prioritize your time, because it lets you be able to have time for most things and realize time waits for no one and you feel better about getting things done.

Keeping track of my time helps me to be more organized and manage my time wisely.

Sometimes there is more time if we plan what to do and set the time to do it.

I am learning to be more time conscious now and to try and make my time count for something.

References

Colvin, R.H., & Taylor, D.D. (1978). Planning student work-study time in an objectives-based medical curriculum. *Journal of Medical Education*, 53, 393-396.

Authors advocate a formula for calculating time necessary for learning activities.

Davis, W.K., & Heller, L.E. (1976). The effects of a demanding curriculum on students' allocation of time. *Journal of Medical Education*, 51, 506-507.

Twenty-eight day study of nineteen sophomore medical students at University of Michigan Medical School. Strong positive correlation between amount of study time and grades. Average total time in personal study and classes was 60 hours.

Garrard, J., Lorents, A., & Chilgren, R. (1972). Student allocation of time in a semioptional medical curriculum. *Journal of Medical Education*, 47:460-466.

Twenty one-day random observations of twenty-one medical students. Students scheduled 31.8 hours per week by the school for organized learning activities. Students recorded a total of 110.96 hours in all activities, including personal time, transit, personal study and patient-related work.

Gupta, S. (March 13, 2006). Your time: Sleep deprived. *Time Magazine*, p. 68.

Dr. Gupta reports on his personal experience of a sleep deprivation experiment.

Howard, P.J. (2nd edition 2000). *The owner's manual for the brain: everyday applications from mind-brain research*. Atlanta: Bard Press.

Chapter 7 is entitled A Good Night's Sleep: Cycles, Drams, Naps and Nightmares and reviews research of each, including the link between sleep and memory and how to promote regular sleeping habits.

Knaus, W. (1997). *Do it now!: Break the procrastination habit*. Hoboken, N.J.: Wiley.

Using the "awareness/action" approach, Knaus shows readers how to identify root causes for procrastination and suggests solutions. One of his more widely known methods is the "five minute rule" where you promise yourself to work for only five minutes on a task you'd prefer to avoid—and then after the first five minutes decide whether to continue or to quit. Most people find they will continue working past the five minute mark.

Mednick, S.C., & Ehrman, M. (2006). *Take a nap! Change your life.* New York: Workman Publishing.

This book discusses the research on the benefits of napping and shows you how to plan the optimum nap to increase alertness, strengthen memory and reduce stress.

Pauk, W. (1997). *How to study in college.* Boston: Houghton Mifflin Company.

Study skills workbook for college students. Has a section on procrastination.

Pychyl, T. (2006). Procrastination Research Group (PRG), Carleton University, Ottawa, Canada, Department of Psychology. Retrieved from http://http-server.carleton.ca/~tpychyl/ index.html

Site originates at Carleton University, but represents a compilation of information and research on procrastination from all over the world.

Spiegel, K., Leproult, R., & Van Cauter, E. (1999). Impact of a sleep debt on metabolic and endocrine function. *The Lancet*, 354, 1435-1439.

Rise in cortisol, also known as the "stress hormone," and slowing of glucose metabolism occur with lack of sleep, even over a short period of time. Elevated cortisol levels have been linked with memory impairment.

Van Cauter, E., Leproult, R., & Plat, L. (2000). Age-related changes in slow wave sleep and REM sleep and relationship with growth hormone and cortisol levels in healthy men. *Journal of the American Medical Association*, 284, 861-868.

Rise in cortisol, also known as the "stress hormone", and slowing of glucose metabolism occur with lack of sleep, even over a short period of time. Elevated cortisol levels have been linked with memory impairment.

Vital Skills

Preread to Get More Out of Lecture and Reading Assignments

(Week 1)

Prereading works!

 Assessment: Preparing For Lecture

Never
Rarely
Sometimes
Often
Always

Directions: Circle the number that most accurately describes your behavior.

0 ①2 3 4   1. Before a lecture I read the text, syllabus or PowerPoint slides to see what will be covered.

0 1 2 ③ 4   2. I know what the main ideas of the lecture topic will be before the lecture begins.

0 1 2 ③ 4   3. I can usually spell all of the key words used in lecture.

0 1 2 ③ 4   4. I can quickly (10-15 minutes) go through a course textbook and pick out the important points.

Never Rarely Sometimes Often Always

0 1 (2) 3 4   5. Even before a lecture begins, I have an idea of what form my lecture notes will take (e.g., if I'll make diagrams, charts, note cards, loose notes.)

4 3 (2) 1 0   6. I am often sleepy during lecture.

(4) 3 2 1 0   7. I spend too much time reworking and rewriting my notes after a lecture.

4 (3) 2 1 0   8. It's hard for me to understand what the lecturer is talking about.

4 (3) 2 1 0   9. I have difficulty concentrating during lecture.

4 (3) 2 1 0   10. There are always a lot of new, unfamiliar vocabulary words used in lecture.

___27___   **Total Score** *(Add the numbers circled)*

Feedback on Preparing for Lecture Answers

1. Since about one third of your study time is spent in lecture, why not make it as profitable as possible? Looking ahead at what will be covered in class is an excellent way to improve your understanding and retention of the lecture and reading assignments.

2. You'll feel so smart knowing what is coming next! Being able to anticipate and predict are two important aspects of critical thinking. You will also be able to ask intelligent questions in class.

3. Note making is a lot easier if you are already familiar with the vocabulary.

4. Being able to pick out the main ideas and related details is another facet of critical thinking. The point of prereading is to RAPIDLY determine the big picture. If you're spending more than 10 minutes, you're reading the text. Reading the text is obviously important, but prereading BEFORE reading is the key to increasing comprehension, retention and reading speed. *As one student said, "Prereading gave the lecture a kind of skeletal structure. It put things in perspective; more like a filing cabinet than a junk-drawer in the kitchen."*

5. It's a real time saver if you can begin making condensed, review notes in class! *A student commented, "I was able to understand clearer and faster because the material was familiar."*

6. Feeling sleepy can have many causes, the chief one being lack of sleep. Not being mentally engaged and challenged can also be a cause. Topics with which you are already familiar will be more interesting. Also, if you have a general idea where the lecturer is going, you will be able to capture the important details in your notes. You're less likely to feel sleepy when you are actively involved in note-making during class.

7. At least half of your study time will be spent making highly organized study notes. Keep in mind that making the notes is an important step in the overall system. Time must also be scheduled

for review and later for self-testing. That's why you made the notes!

8. Knowing the key topics in advance permits you to put the bits and pieces of a rambling lecture into the right format. Having some knowledge beforehand will help you ask clarifying questions, which does NOT include, "Will this be on the test?"

9. You do not get so easily lost during lecture if you have a road map based on prereading. Being engaged in the topic and discussion will help you concentrate.

10. If you have preread, then the vocabulary is likely to be familiar. Since you won't have to stop and ponder "what does that mean?" you'll be able to get a better set of notes and your reading speed and comprehension will improve. *One student said, "I don't feel so lost in class."*

Score Interpretation: Preparing for Lecture

A score of 30 or higher is very good. **Great job!**

A score of 29 or lower means you could get more "bang for your study buck" by prereading. Give it a try!

 # Goal: Prepare For Lecture

The goal of prereading is to increase your understanding and retention of material presented in lecture, to increase reading speed and comprehension, and to accelerate your note-making.

 **Rationale**

How to Get the Most of Out of Lectures

Many students don't know how to make the best use of lecture time. You have surely noticed classmates who are asleep, half-asleep, text-messaging friends, checking e-mails or just thinking about something completely unrelated to the lecture.

"Classes are a lot more interesting
when you know what is going on!"

Though lectures may not be the most efficient method for conveying information (textbooks usually are), they offer at least five advantages.

Five Benefits of Attending Lectures

1. Gives you an idea of what the instructor thinks is important (and therefore likely to be on the test)

2. Imposes order on the information (from the handouts and/or the lecture itself)

3. Provides an auditory mode of input (hearing it)

4. Adds the most recent information that has not yet made it to the textbooks

5. Presents an opportunity to ask questions about something that is unclear to you and to hear the questions of other students.

If you are familiar with the material *before* lecture, it is much easier to pick out the patterns that emerge from the information. Structuring the information according to these patterns is a very important step in the learning process.

The main sources you will use for prereading are:

- Course textbooks,
- Course syllabi and objectives,
- PowerPoint slides or other handouts.

How often a topic is mentioned in any of these sources is an indicator of its importance and the likelihood, therefore, of its appearance later on a test. Anything that is mentioned in all three resources (four, including the lecture itself) you can count on seeing again—on an exam. Whatever form your notes take (See Chapter 4), the more important concepts and details definitely need to be featured prominently.

Close attention will help you will figure out what is important to each of your lecturers. Instructors typically cover in lecture about 70% of what they plan to ask on the exam.

Here are some tips to help you learn to "read" your instructors:

- If they want to make sure you are reading the text, sometimes they will purposefully not mention something in lecture but will direct you to the assigned reading material.

- Lecturers will sometimes mention a general topic during lecture and then, when writing the exam questions, will ask a specific detail about that topic which is found only in the text or handouts.

- After the instructors and course director go to all the trouble of creating the course objectives, they are very likely to return to them for test items.

- The number of times a concept is mentioned will help you gauge its importance to the lecturer. Does he or she always bring up how the topic would apply to pediatric cases? Take note.

Prereading Is the Key to Getting the Most Out Of Lecture

While preparing for lecture can certainly consist of *more* than prereading (some diligent students preread, read and make notes before attending each lecture—highly commendable!), we believe that prereading is the *least* you should do before attending a lecture.

Students who preread can testify to its value in understanding the lecture:

I knew what the lecturer was talking about.
I could spell the words in my notes.
I asked great questions.
I was well prepared.
The topic was familiar. I didn't feel lost.

There are other benefits to prereading, too. When you return to read the text more thoroughly after prereading, studies have shown you will increase your reading speed by 25% and increase your comprehension by at least 10%. Talk about efficient!

What Is Prereading?

- **Skimming.** If it takes more than 10-15 minutes to preread, you're not prereading. You'll know the difference between reading and prereading by how much time it takes. Fast, fast, fast!

- **Looking for the main idea(s).** What is the "big picture"?

- Becoming familiar with the **vocabulary** and learning **new terms or abbreviations** that will be used in the lecture. You can highlight them, or better yet, make vocabulary cards.

- **Discovering patterns.** Look for relationships. How do the subtopics relate to the main concept? How many important details do there seem to be? (numbered lists with details about each item, comparison, contrast). Look for clusters of information. There will be more about this in the next chapter.

- What kind of information is it? **Analyzing** whether it is cause and effect, the steps in a process, a diagram with structures to remember, classification, etc. Chapter 4 will give more detailed explanation about this type of analysis.

 How a textbook is arranged will give you clues as to what the authors think is important.

Getting Acquainted With Your Textbook

Since you will be spending at least the next semester and perhaps the next year with each of your texts, why not get to know them and learn what they have to offer?

Each textbook is designed to have a different approach to the information and will often include study aids. Go ahead and break the seal on the CD that came with your book! Some of them are very helpful. Once you are familiar with all the tools at hand, you will quickly be able to tell when to use each one.

Take a minute and drag out one of your heavy text books. Flip through the Table of Contents. That is the Very Big Picture. Are there any interesting looking entries? Turn to the back of the book. Is there an Index? What type of information is listed there? Are there any Appendices? What is included in those? Is there a CD? What material does that contain? Have you visited the publisher's website? Does the site have chapter outlines or sample test questions? Now that you know these are available, you will be prepared to use them wisely.

Some of you may be thinking, "If a little bit is good, then even more is better!" Hold on. Do NOT attempt to use every study aid for every course! Find out what study aids are available and then choose the one or two that are most useful for that particular course.

How To Preread

You may preread from a variety of materials:

- Course textbooks,
- Course syllabus,
- PowerPoint slides or other handouts,
- Review books.

You can't preread from every source available, so you'll need to choose the best one (or two) for each class.

What To Look At When You Are Prereading

- Study questions—read these first (they will point to what the authors think is the most important information),

- Summary—read this next (brief overview of the whole chapter).

Then quickly flip through the pages in the chapter and notice:

- Main headings,
- Bold-faced print,
- Boxed information,
- Diagrams and pictures,
- Charts, tables, graphs.

When you preread you are interacting with the text instead of being a passive bystander. This active engagement helps you remember information longer.

Critical thinking is part of active learning. It includes asking questions as you read:

- What is the main point?
- How are the details related to the main point?
- What patterns can I detect?

When to Preread

Students often find it difficult to preread immediately before a lecture when classes are scheduled back-to-back. So when should you preread? The best time is often the evening before the next day's lectures. Another option is to get up a few minutes earlier in the morning and preread for that day's classes. Find the time that works best for you and then stick with it. These few minutes of preparation will very quickly pay big dividends!

Building Your Medical Vocabulary

Work on increasing your medical vocabulary as you preread. Keep a stack of blank note cards or sheet of paper at hand. You can quickly jot down unfamiliar words as you see them and write out the definitions either while you preread or before lecture.

Prereading SAVES time. It:

- helps you to understand and absorb more from lecture,
- speeds up reading and
- gets you started on making study notes more quickly.

 **Interventions**

Exercise 1 — Prereading Trial Run

Choose a chapter from any book that will be covered in lecture in the next few days (preferably tomorrow). Check your watch or timer and give yourself no more than 10 minutes to preread the section you've chosen. Count the number of pages before you begin, so you'll know how to pace yourself. Return to Check-Up for Exercise #1, below, when you've finished.

Guidelines for the Prereading Exercise

- Set a timer for the allotted time. (No more than 10 minutes.)

- Put both hands on your book or other reading material. Have one hand ready to turn the page.

- Give yourself a purpose for your reading and a reason to remember what you've read. The objectives in your course syllabus will be a good guide here.

- Look for the general concepts, not the details.

- Look for cues that indicate most important ideas and terms (use of color, headlines, indentations, outlines, italics, bold, underlining).

- Move your eyes down the page quickly. You should feel a slight tension about getting through this material in the time you've allowed.

 **Evaluation**

Check-Up for Exercise 1 — Prereading
Trial Run

1. What were the main points or topics in the
    chapter or section you preread?

    _____

    _____

    _____

    _____

2. If there were several points or topics, how do they
    relate to each other?

    _____

    _____

    _____

    _____

3. Do you remember any of the details? How do
    they relate to the main point?

    _____

    _____

    _____

Even though most students do not currently preread before
class, studies (and common sense) have shown that
prereading will increase your understanding and help you
remember the information for a longer period of time. By
prereading you can figure out what is important, get better
lecture notes and recall information more easily on tests.

CHAPTER 3

Some students find it helpful to think of prereading like this. Pretend you are in a restaurant that has a long, long lunch buffet. Prereading is like walking along the buffet to see what your choices are, before you pick up a plate and start putting food on it.

Prereading is getting "the lay of the land" (or buffet) so you can make informed choices when you read, listen to the lecture and make notes.

 You'll be pleasantly surprised how much more you get out of lecture when you preread.

Exercise 2 — Incorporate Prereading in Your Schedule: Actually Prereading

Your assignment for this week is to preread for at least one of your more difficult classes each day. You can either preread for morning lectures the previous night, or get up a bit earlier and preread that morning. You may want to preread for afternoon classes during your lunch break. The idea is to have the information fresh in your brain when you attend the lecture.

Complete the exercise below after you have preread for one week.

Check-Up for Exercise 2 — One Week of Prereading

How did prereading affect your lecture experience?

_____

_____

_____

Summary

Prereading is the first step in our 5-step study system.

Students who preread:

- learn more from the lectures,
- remember the information longer,
- can actively participate in class discussions,
- are able to read the text faster,
- are able to make study notes more quickly.

Student Feedback

I knew more in-depth what the professor was talking about and was able to spend less time reading.

You know when a topic starts and when it ends. It gives you an idea as to what the discussion is all about.

It worked! I got some useful insights and knew where the lecture was going.

Our program requires us to read the text before lecture and the teachers often give pop quizzes. If you're not prepared for lecture then you won't understand it as well, and you'll be embarrassed if you are called on in class and don't know the answer.

I understood what was going on. Could find things in the book and knew exactly what she was talking about! It also helped me make a good grade on the quiz.

Because you understand it better after prereading and lecture, you spend less time studying for a test.

I preread for my nursing fundamentals course. We had a quiz that I feel I was well prepared for.

It helps me to know what the topic is all about, what to expect from the lecture and I know the main points of the topic.

Prereading gave me familiarity with and recognition of the material covered. It also gave me confidence because of being familiar with the material. It really helps increase the speed at which you learn.

I was able to picture (inside my head) what was being discussed in lecture. I was also more focused in class.

Prereading prevents me from being totally lost during the lecture. Knowing some things about the lecture keeps me from being bored and uninvolved.

After prereading for my classes in the first year of nursing school, I discovered that I had built up such a good database that I didn't have to preread for all my classes in the second year. Now I just preread when a new or really difficult topic is being taught.

 References

Cook, L.K., & Mayer, R.E. (1988). Teaching readers about the structure of a scientific text. *Journal of Educational Psychology*, 80, 448-456.

> College biology students showed substantial gains in recall of high conceptual information when they had previously noted the organization of information presented in the text: enumeration, sequence, or comparison and contrast.

Jacobowitz, T. (1981). The effects of modified skimming on college students' recall and recognition of expository text. *Directions in Reading: Research and Instruction*. The National Reading Conference, Inc., Washington, D.C., pp. 232-237.

> Advance knowledge of the text facilitates understanding. Skimming provides insight into the text by exposing the reader to many of the major points intended by the author.

Karlin, R. (1969). *Reading for achievement.* New York: Holt, Rinehart, Winston, Inc.

Provides detailed instructions on pages 3-25 on how to preread.

Krug, D., George, B., Hannon, S.A., & Glover, J.A. (1989). The effect of outlines and headings on readers' recall of text. *Contemporary Educational Psychology,* 14 (2),111-123.

Students who read outlines prior to reading the texts recall information better on later tests.

Quirk, M.E. (1994). *How to learn and teach in medical school.* Springfield, MA: Charles E. Thomas.

Strongly recommends previewing for meaning prior to reading and gives instructions on previewing skills.

Redding, R.E. (1990). Metacognitive instruction: Trainers teaching thinking skills. *Performance Improvement Quarterly,* 3 (1), 27-41.

Review of research in critical thinking skills.

Snapp, J.C., & Glover J.A. (1990). Advance organizers and study questions. *Journal of Educational Research,* 83 (51), 266-271.

Students who preread the text, or had an overview, gave significantly better answers to higher order study questions.

Spencer, F., Johnston, M., & Ames, W. (1981). The effect of manipulating the advance organizer and other prereading strategies on comprehension of abstract text. *Directions in Reading: Research and Instruction.* The National Reading Conference, Inc., Washington, D.C., pp. 228-231.

Prereading can significantly increase the processing of unfamiliar or abstract material, especially if the material is not well organized.

Tudor, I. (1986). Advance organisers as adjuncts to reading comprehension. *Journal of Research in Reading,* 9 (2), 103-115.

Experiment showed advance organizers, that is, prereading, facilitates comprehension especially for more complex texts. The greater the level of textual difficulty, the more benefit advance organizers provide.

CHAPTER 3

Wade, S.E., Reynolds, R.E. (1989). Developing metacognitive awareness. *Journal of Reading*, 33 (1), 6-14.

Deciding what to study, or "what is important," is a key component to skillful reading. Skilled learners pay extra attention to main ideas of the text and are aware of textual clues that point to key ideas. The clues are headings, topic sentences, amount of space author gives to the idea, bold-face type, italics, lists and study questions provided.

Making Organized Study Notes

(Week 2)

> *The information is now very familiar. I can still recall the information easily, and I took the test weeks ago!*

✓ Assessment: Note-Making

Never
Rarely
Sometimes
Often
Always

Directions: *Circle the number that best describes your actual behavior during an academic term.*

4 3 ②1 0   1. I highlight important information in the textbook, which can be as much as a third of each page.

0 1 ②3 4   2. Immediately after lecture, while the information is fresh in my mind, I rewrite/reorganize my notes.

4 3 ②1 0   3. I don't "get" some of what I read.

0 1 2 ③4   4. I keep paper and pencil handy and make notes while I read.

0 1 2 ③4   5. I put my notes into condensed format, as cards, charts, diagrams, or outlines, for later review before tests.

Never	Rarely	Sometimes	Often	Always		

0 1 2 3 (4)   6. I make certain that my organized notes relate the details of the text to the main ideas, as presented in lecture and in the text.

0 1 2 3 (4)   7. My notes are in a format designed for quick and easy review.

0 1 2 (3) 4   8. My notes are organized so I can test my self on them before an exam.

0 1 (2) 3 4   9. When my self-testing shows that I have not retained an important detail, I put that detail on a flash card and review until I have memorized it.

(4) 3 2 1 0   10. I lose the "big picture" and get lost in the details.

0 1 2 3 (4)   11. I see how details fit into the main themes of the topic I'm studying.

0 1 2 3 (4)   12. I use visual cues to make relationships among details "pop up" in my notes.

___38___   **Total Score** *(Add up the answers to get your score.)*

Continue after you have calculated your score on the Note-Making Assessment.

Feedback on Note-Making Answers

1. "Rainbow books" may look pretty but aren't very useful. Highlighting is okay for marking main ideas, some of the important details or vocabulary

words but can't be used efficiently for review or self-test. If a lot of the text is highlighted or underlined, there will be too much material to review. Also, highlighting does not help put details in the context of main ideas. Finally, authors of textbooks usually already have "highlighted" the main topics and details by use of larger type fonts and colored ink.

2.   Rewriting and organizing your notes within a day of the lecture ensures that you will always be caught up and will not have to "cram" before an exam. Also, it is best to make your notes while the information from the lecture and reading is still fresh and vivid in your thoughts. Put it on your schedule!

3.   If you're thinking, "I don't understand," you need to go through the process of making very organized notes in order to see the relationships among the details presented. You are probably just getting lost in the details. But if there really is a complex concept to conquer, help is on the way. See "Seven Steps to Better Understanding" later in this chapter.

4.   The goal of note-making is to eliminate having to refer to the textbook itself. We want you to get the information into a highly organized, compact form that you can review repeatedly and use for self-testing. Making notes on a separate sheet of paper or in a notebook as you read your textbooks is the first step toward creating that excellent set of notes. (*One student tells of having car trouble on the way home the evening before a big exam. All she had with her were the charts and note cards she had made, no textbook or other study materials. While waiting (several hours) for the tow truck to arrive she*

reviewed the notes she had with her. She arrived home late at night and fell exhausted into bed. The next morning she got up and rushed off to take the test, hoping and praying that her notes had been complete enough. While taking the exam, she felt confident that she had studied the right material, and she was right. She ACED it!)

5. Condensing your notes into outlines, tables, charts, diagrams, or cards calls for analysis of the nature of the information to be learned. Is the information a list to be remembered? Does it consist of main topics with a series of sub-topics that are similar in some way? Does the information occur in a sequence? Is it primarily visual, like a diagram? This analysis is the "big picture," what experts on learning call "metacognition." Research shows that metacognition (perceiving the nature of the information to be learned) and contextual organization are keys to understanding and recall.

6. Many students have told us that learning to make a set of highly organized, condensed notes was the most useful study skill they ever acquired (after learning to spend enough time studying). Why? Because it forced them to think about the structure of the information to be learned, and it made review and self-test easy.

7. Repetition. Repetition. Repetition. It can't be said too often: Repetition is the key to memory. Make it your motto. If you create condensed notes in a format that you can review easily, you will be able to review your notes more often.

8. How can you know what you know and don't

CHAPTER 4

Vital Skills

know? How can you know if you are ready for a test? The same way an athlete knows when she is ready for an event. Think of yourself as a test-taking athlete. No athlete would enter a 100-yard dash without having practiced running it many, many, many times! To know what you don't know (yet), you need to test yourself over the material in advance of the classroom exam. So, your condensed, organized notes must be in a format for self-testing. As you self-test, you can zero in on the information you don't know and put it on flash cards for further review. That way you don't need to keep reviewing the whole body of information, just the parts that require further attention. Efficient!

9. The beauty of flash cards is their portability (they fit easily into your bag, pocket or purse) and they are easy to sort, even in odd bits of time, such as waiting for class to begin or during a break. As you go through your set of cards, you can sort them into "know" and "don't know" piles, which allows you to continually spend your time on what you *don't* know. Reviewing them often during the day will help you remember important details your self-testing showed you do not yet recall easily.

10. This will not happen once you acquire the habit of making good study notes. Good notes relate the details to the main ideas. Getting "lost in the details" usually means you are trying to learn them out of the context of the bigger picture.

11. Good! Keeping the over-all picture in mind helps you organize and remember the significant details. For example, the big picture may be "Diseases of the Liver." So, each disease listed is important.

What are the important details about each disease? And so on...

12. You want to be able to review your notes quickly, so you can go over them repeatedly in the time available. Visual aids (use of color, boxes) allow you to get your eyes over your notes rapidly. We've found that many of our students actually enjoy making, and take pride in, their notes, because they are interesting and colorful.

Score Interpretation — Note-Making

40-48 =   Very good.
24-39 =   Good but could use improvement.
Below 24 = This chapter can really, really help you!

No matter what your score you will definitely learn something useful in this chapter. Good note makers can become GREAT note makers! We'll show you how to organize your notes so the details are easy to keep straight.

> *Making my own study notes helped me to see the information in a different way. It's so much easier to remember, since I made the notes myself!*

 ## Goal: How to Choose the Best Note Format

The goal of this chapter is to teach you the most effective way to organize your notes for ease in studying and recalling massive amounts of detailed information and to show you how to choose the best note-making format.

The Learning Process

Learning in nursing school is a continuum which begins with prereading, proceeds through reading and making organized notes, continues with reviewing and self-testing and culminates with the application of knowledge on a test or in nursing practice. *(See the flowchart below.)*

Vital Skills in the Learning Process

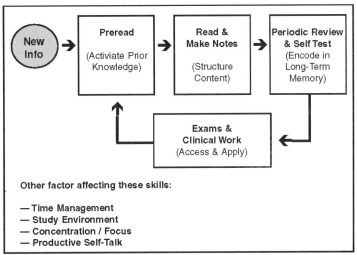

Figure 4.1

This chapter will present specific research-based methods of structuring the material which will enable you to more easily understand the information and also more easily store the information in your long-term memory.

Use of Computers for Taking Notes in Class

Many students take their laptop computers to class and play stenographer during lecture. But those same students tell us that they really aren't able to pay attention to what the instructor is saying while busily inputting everything that is said.

If you use your computer to take notes, we recommend that you do not get caught up in trying to format everything as you type, but that you simply record the most important points made by the lecturer. Immediately after class you will need to make time to organize the notes and fill in any gaps. Organizing the notes afterwards will also help you better understand the material that was presented in class.

The other option is to go back to the plain old pen and paper method to take notes. There is something beneficial in the kinesthetic process of actually writing things down that you just can't experience when using a keyboard.

If you're prereading before you go to class, you will already have a good idea of where the lecture will go, and it will be simple enough to take notes of the important topics. Reading the text later will help you fill in any gaps before you make your final set of notes—either on the computer or in your own handwriting.

 **Rationale**

It's All in the Details

Once upon a time you were probably able to do just fine in class simply by attending lecture and never cracking open a book. In other classes you may have had to read the text as well as listen to the lecture and maybe jot down a few notes. In yet another class perhaps you really had to "get serious" and do some highlighting as you read the text and maybe even write a few notes in a notebook. If it was a REALLY difficult class you might have had to try and organize the notes in an outline or some other form so you could look back over them again the night before an exam.

Those days are over. Welcome to Nursing School!

We have yet to meet a student who feels she was truly well-prepared for the level of detail nursing students are required to know.

What to Include in Your Study Notes

How will you choose what to put in your notes? You will be drawing from a variety of sources, primarily:

- required textbooks
- course syllabus and objectives
- instructor handouts/downloads
- lecture notes

From all that information, what should be included in your notes? If information is included in two of these sources, make sure it is in your notes. If it is in three or more of these sources, be sure it's in your notes in a *memorable way*. You can be fairly certain you will be asked to recall it again—either on a classroom exam or the NCLEX.

Let's Talk About Highlighting

"When you highlight only small sections, it is easier to see what is important."

Some students consider highlighting a form of note-making. Sorry, but it isn't. When you highlight one word or phrase, it says, "Look at me!" But when you highlight most of a page, you have too much information clamoring for your attention. "Look at me!" "No! Look at me!" "Hey! What about me?" "Over here!" "Don't forget about me!"

Too much highlighting makes it hard to see what is truly important.

The key is to use highlighting sparingly, so you can hear it "calling to you." The best highlighters are very selective in what they mark. Vocabulary words are good to highlight. Important ideas that you see repeatedly can be highlighted. You may also want to highlight a detail or concept in your charts.

You may wonder, "Okay, highlighting may not be enough, but why can't I make notes like I always have? Why do I need a set of what you call highly organized and condensed notes?"

Glad you asked!

Here's Why You Should Make a Great Set of Notes

- Your busy schedule just doesn't allow repeated reading of the text—even if it's only what you highlighted. Highly organized notes set you free from your textbooks and can be reviewed quickly and repeatedly. (Remember, repetition is the key to memory.)

- The act of creating your own set of structured notes makes the information your own. What makes it your own is your analysis of what is important, and how the details relate to the main topics.

- You can't really self-test from highlighted passages,

notes made in the margins of the books or from your handouts. You need to be able to self-test, because self-testing lets you know if you're prepared for an exam—or not.

Rules for Making a Good Set of Study Notes

- Include **all essential information** on the topic.

- **Organize** the notes into a format that shows the relationship between topics, subtopics and details.

- Make it **visually interesting**.

- **Condense** material to permit repeated review.

- Use a format which facilitates **self-testing**.

"Now where did I write that down???"

Four Major Note Types

Cards

You probably are already making note cards, but are you using them in the best way? Cards are primarily helpful for repeated review of simple details, for example, vocabulary words and their definitions or short lists. Other notes types are better suited for more complex information.

In case you're not already making cards in the best way, here's a quick review.

- Use both sides of the cards. One side will be for the question, the other for the answer.

- Keep it simple. Too much information makes cards hard to review.

Example of a note card

```
Name the 4
major types of cirrhosis
```

Front

```
1.   Alcholic
2.   Postnecrotic
3.   Biliary
4.   Cardiac
```

Back

It's easy to self test with cards and you can carry them with you anywhere.

> *I'm a confirmed card carrier!*

How to Use Your Note Cards

You can group cards by subject, using a rubber band or putting them on a ring to hold them together. Some students choose to use different colored cards for each topic or class. For example your Pathophysiology cards could be yellow, your Pharmacology cards could be blue, etc.

To self-test from note cards, you simply read the question (or cue) on one side, then say, think or write the answer and turn the card over to check if you were right.

If you answered correctly, put the card in your "know" pile. If not, then it goes into the "don't know" pile. Keep sorting through the "don't know" pile until all cards are all transferred to the "know" pile. This method will keep you from spending time on information you have already mastered.

Always carry 10 or 20 cards from your "don't know" stack. You can do many quick reviews during the day. For example, between classes or while waiting for something or someone. You can easily work in four or five reviews during the day. That night you can happily put all the cards in your "know" pile!

At this rate, you will have mastered 50-100 new details by the end of the week. During a 15-week semester that could add up to 700-1500 factoids!

Keep in mind that several quick review sessions are much better for long term retention than one long "slog."

Advantages of Cards	Disadvantages of Cards
Easy to capture discrete bits of information you must master.	Lose the context, as it is not embedded in a larger picture.
Easy to make.	Some students get "carried away" and try to make all their notes on cards. Not a good idea.
Easy to sort and use for self-testing.	
Portable. You can carry them in a pocket.	

Category Charts

Category charts are so useful in the medical sciences that they are frequently used in textbooks to summarize information. Students tell us that teachers sometimes prepare charts as handouts.

When the task is to *compare and contrast* information, category charts are the way to go. Often there are between three and seven subtopics and then the same number of details for each of those subtopics.

If you needed to know more detail about the four types of cirrhosis, used as an example in the section on note cards, you could make a category chart.

In a typical chart, the names you need to remember are placed in the far left column and the details are placed in boxes across the top row.

4 Types of Cirrhosis	Etiology	How Diagnosed	Prognosis
Alcoholic	Alcohol abuse	Liver biopsy, history of ETOH abuse, AST, high bilirubin, anemia	Depends on complications and continued abuse.
Post-necrotic	Post acute viral Hepatitis types B & C, post intoxication with industrial chemicals, some infections and metabolic disorders	Needle biopsy	75% die of complications.
Biliary	Cause unknown. Chronic stasis of bile and intrahepatic ducts. Autoimmune process implicated.	Elevated serum bilirubin Early = 3-10 mg / 100 ml Late = > 50 mg / 100 ml	None listed in text.
Cardiac	Atrioventricular valve disease. Constrictive pericarditis.	↑ conjugated bilirubin in serum ↑ sulfobromophthalein ↑ serum aminotransferases ↓ albumin in serum	Depends on the course of cardiac disease.

As you can see, there is a major difference between the amount of information on a note card and on a category chart. How can you decide whether the information deserves just a note card, or if a category chart is a better choice? One way to determine if the added details are important is whether they appear in *two* or more of the resources: Textbook, lecture, course objectives or handouts.

   Hint: If your instructors took the time to include the information in your course syllabus, objectives, or handout, you should probably make a chart.

Advantages of Category Charts	Disadvantages of Category Charts
Show the relationship between main ideas and details.	Take longer to make than loose notes, because you have to think about the organization. But, really, that's a good thing.
Provide a context in which to remember the details. Context aids understanding and recall.	
Review is simple, especially compared to re-reading the text.	
Possible to self-test yourself over a lot of information.	
Visual impoact of the chart makes it, and its content, memorable. Some students say they can picture the whole chart in their mineds during an exam and find the correct answer to a question.	

"Take time to admire your work."

Examples of Students' Charts

Following are some student-made charts which show how other nursing students have organized the information they need to learn. These study aids may give you ideas on how you might want to make your own notes.

Warning: There may be factual errors in these sample charts, so do not plan to use them for your own studies without first checking them for accuracy. Also note that these students use their own short-hand to save space, e.g., ↓ for decrease, ↑ for increase, SE for side effects, etc.

Note how these charts are organized. Do you see why the student chose the particular structure? Your own charts may be organized differently from these examples. That's fine. These are personalized and individualized learning tools. They should make sense to *you* and help *you* remember what's important to know.

Analgesia & Anesthetics in Pre-Partum Care

Name	Route	Mom Side Effects	Fetal Side Effects	Nursing Implications	Other
Morphine Sulfate	IM IV *(fast! < 1m)* Epidural (peak 10 m - 1 hr)	• → CNS (resp) • → Uterine activity N&V, pruritis • N&V • pruritis	→ in FHR variability → CNS (resp) Hypotonia (flaccid muscles)	• Common i / 1st stage of prodromal labor to induce sleep • Be aware of peak effects	Analgesic
Meperidine HCl (Demerol)	IM IV *(few mins)*	• → CNS (resp) • Hypotension • N&V, blurry vision • Drowsy • → in contractility (mild)	→ in FHR variability → CNS (resp) Hypotonia (flaccid muscles) Lethargy < 79 hrs (post)	• Admin in ACTIVE phase • IV push slowly over 3-5m • Resp < 12, call dr • Do NOT give if del imminent • Keep narc antagonist to neonate if depression evident	Analgesic *make sure to time meds w / ctxs or baby gets meds!*
Nalbuphine HCl (Nubain)	IM IV *(2-3m)*	• CNS sedation (dizzy, vertigo) • Resp depress • Hypotension • N&V, dry mouth, blurry vision • Diaphoresis	→ in FHR variability Resp depression	• Do not admin to narc depend women • Admin IV over 3-5m • Resp < 12, call dr	Analgesic
Butorphanol (Stadol)	IM IV *(few mins)*	• Resp depress • Blurry vision • Dry mouth • Drowsy • Hypotension • N&V *withdrawal i / drug dependent women*	Resp depression	• Do not admin to narc depend women • Use Narcan to reverse infant effect • Resp < 12, call dr	Analgesic

Chart provided by R. Mistry / Texas Woman's University

Chart 4.1

Anesthetics Table

Name	Site	Effect	Advantages	Disadvantages	RN to do
Pudendal Block	Pudendal nerve near ischial spine	5-6 inch / 22 gauge Numbs vagina & perineum *can be combined with inhaled agent	• Safe • One shot to each side • Pt conscious • Pt able to feel ctxs • No pt HypoTN	• Mins before loss of sensation • Allergic rxn • Pt must be cooperative • Needle is *scary* • ↰Pain sensation in perineum	• R / O hx of prev rxn • Give support • Prevent viewing of needles
Saddle Block *"Subarachnoid"*	*into* SF of subarachnoid space	Numbs lower body (i.e., if riding saddle, all places that would have contact w / it) **give btwn ctxs Can be given in 2nd or 3rd phase	• Quick • Safe • Pt conscious • ⊘ N&V	• Potential intro of contaminants to SF • Neuro sequela • Ability to push altered • Slows labor • Resp. paralysis • *Post Spinal* headache • Inability to void • Systemic toxic rxn	• Pt must sit for 60-90s aft receiving • Aseptic technique • Place hand on fundus (palpate ctxs) to tell pt when to push • Assist w ambulation
Peridural Block *"Continuous Lumbar Epidural"*	Into epidural space ***Can be given i/1st phase of later phases of labor *dura NOT punctured* ⊘ SF leakage	Numbs lower body	• Can start i/1st stage • Pt alert • ↰Exhaustion • Pleasant exp • Control HTN • Used i/premie labor, pre-eclamp, & pts w/labor requiring minimal effort on their behalf	• Pt ⊘ push • Pt HypoTN • Fetal hypoxia • Slows labor • ↰Urge to void	• Keep ephedrine readily available • ✓ for *HypoTN* • Give O_2 • Elevate legs

ADD & ADHD / CNS Drug Therapy

Name	Mechanism of Action	Indications	Pharmacokinetics	SE / AE	Nursing Management
atomoxetine (Strattera)	1st non controlled	ADHD	Dose 1.2-2 mg / D Selectively inhibits reuptake of norepinephrine	Abdominal pain, constipation, weight loss, irritability, mood swings, dry mouth, nausea, insomnia, anorexia	Symptoms not as severe as Ritalin
methylphenidate hydrochloride (Ritalin)	Pharmacodynamics unclear Mild CNS stimulant *Drug Interactions:* CNS stimulants > CV reactions, nervousness, insomnia, consulsions MAOI > HA, dysrhythmias, vomiting, HTN meperidine — severe resp. depression, seizures, hypotension, CV collapse, death tricyclic — > dysrhythmias, tachycardia, HTN	Narcolepsy ADD	Absorbed in GI Metabolized: liver Excreted: Kidney ½ life 2 hrs *Contraindications:* Cardiac disease, HTN, hyperthyroidism, glaucoma, hx of drug abuse *Caution:* epilepsy, emotionally unstable, pregnancy	Insomnia, restlessness, liver dysfunction, anorexia, headache, drowsiness, tachycardia, HTN, chest pain, rash, fever, > bruising	*Toxicity:* Confusion, delirium, dry mouth, euphoria, severe headache, HTN, tremors, muscle twitch, arrhythmias, vomiting, convulsions, coma *Toxicity Tx:* Supportive: emesis / gastric lavage / short acting barbiturate (i.e., Seconal) *Monitor:* weight, growth D / C periodically Drug holiday when low stress *Instruct:* Take 30-45" ac, 6 hr before hs, SR swallowed whole, do not ↑dosage or stop abruptly, will not solve ed / social problems, ongoing involvement necessary, *do not take any other drug, esp.* OTC

Chart 4.3

Created by D. Griffith — University of Texas Health Science Center — Houston

Muscle Relaxants / CNS Drug Therapy

Drug Name	Mechanism of Action	Indications	Pharmacokinetics	SE / AE	Nursing Management
baclofen (Lioresal)	Central acting Mechanism unknown	MS Spinal Cord injuries *Caution:* hepatic / renal dysfunction, pregnant women, older adults, epilepsy	Absorption: variable PO Onset: hr-weeks PO Peak: 2-3 hrs ½ life 2.5-4 hrs *Therapeutic serum level 80-400 mg / ml* Adult 5-80 mg PO tid	Drowsiness, vertigo, confusion, sleepiness, weakness, blurred vision, lethargy, nausea, *hyperglycemia (adj: insulin)* *Contraindications:* Hypersensitivity	*Drug Interactions:* ETOH, CNS depressants > Dosage gradually to therapeutic levels Gradual reduction over 2 weeks Maximum benefit 1-2 months Caution: Driving & using machinery Adm w/ food Tabs may be crushed
dantrolene (Dantrium)	Central acting Inhibits release of calcium (Acts directly on skeletal muscles)	Malignant hyperthermia MS Cerebral palsy Spinal cord insults CVA	PO Onset: > week PO Peak: 5 hrs PO ½ life > 8 hrs Metabolized: liver Excreted: kidneys IV ½ life: 4-8 hrs *PO: May mix w / fruit juice, adm immediately after mixing.* *IV: Reconstitute w / 60 ml sterile water, shake until clear, use w / in 6 hrs; incompatible w / acidic solutions (5% D NS)*	Diarrhea, dizziness, sleepiness, fatigue, muscle weakness, N / V, resp. difficulty, depression *Contraindications:* Hepatic disease Women > 35 (if HRT) *Caution:* Impaired cardiac, hepatic, pulmonary fuction, lactose intolerance *Photosensitivity — Avoid sun*	*Drug Interactions:* CCBs (CV collapse) ETOH / CNS depressants (> CNS depression) Hepatotoxic drugs (liver toxicity) *Monitor:* *Hepatitis* 3-12 months Diarrhea Constipation Spasticity Malignant hyperthermia — anesthesia d / c, oxygen, metabolic acidosis, F&E corrected, pt cooled

Chart 4.4

Making Organized Study Notes

Renal Disorders

Renal Disorder	Etiology	Clinical Manifestations (Pathophysiology)	Nursing Management
Goodpasture syndrome (acute Glomerulo-nephritis)	Autoimmune disorder where Ab against the structures of the glomeruli are produced (see pg 1) Rapid progressive Glomerulonephritis Can have life-threatening lung bleeding	May be mild & detected through a UA or hx of pharyngitis or tonsillitis w / fever Headache Malaise Facial edema Proteinuria (mos) Flank pain & / or CVA tenderness Microscopic hematuria (mos) *Complications:* HTN encephalopathy CHF Pulmonary edema May progress to Chronic	Plasmapheresis (filter out Ab) Immunosuppressive agents (prednisone) If residual strep, tx w / PCN Bedrest during accute phase until urine clears, BUN, creatinine, and BP normal Dietary PRO restriction when renal insufficiency present and ↑ BUN Na restriction—↓ BP; edema, CHF Diuretics & anti-HTN agents may be used to control BP CHO given liberally for energy & reduce catabo-lism of PRO Monitor I & O closely Daily wt. monitor for s / s dehydration (diuresis begins 1-2 wks after onset of symptoms)
CRF Glomerulo-nephritis	May progress from acute or may represent a milder type of Ag-Ab reaction Can have repeated occur-rences reducing the kidneys to 1/5 normal size & mostly fibrous Results in ESRD	May be discovered accidentally: ↑ BUN & creatinine, HTN Routine eye exam w/vascular changes & retinal hemorrhages found *General Symptoms:* Feel slightly swollen at night, loss of wt & strength, ↑ irritability, nocturia, headaches, dizziness, digestive problems *Progression:* (S / S renal insufficiency & CRF): Appear poorly nourished w / yellow-gray pigmentation of skin, periorbital & peripheral edema, ↑BP, retinal hemorrhages, mucous membranes pale (anemia), ↓JVD (fluid overload), dyspnea, cardiomegaly & other CHF s / s, crackles, pericarditis (w / friction rub & pulsus paradoxus), late stage: peripheral neuropathies w / loss of deep tendon reflexes	Manage HTN—Na & H2O restrict PRO of ↑biologic value (animal) Adequate calories Antibiotics if UTI Edema—bedrest, HOB elevated, wt. daily, diuretics Dialysis

Created by D. Griffith, The University of Texas Health Science Center — Houston

Chart 4.5

Metabolic Acidosis & Alkalosis Chart

	pH	CO²	HCO³
Respiratory Acid	←	→	OK
Respiratory Alkaline	→	←	OK
Metabolis Acid	←	OK	←
Metabolic Alkaline	→	OK	→

Created by L. DeBow-Platt, RN, Texas Children's Hospital — Houston, TX

Chart 4.6

General Review Chart

System or Disease	Pathophysiological Process	Early & Late Manifestations	Most Important or Life-Threatening Complications	Medical Treatment	Prioritize Nursing Interventions Associated with Early / Late Manifestations	What Nurse Teaches Client / Family to Prevent or Adapt to Disease

Column titles from Successful Problem-Solving & Test-Taking for Beginning Nursing Students, Hoefler, P.A.

Chart 4.7

Tips on Making Your Own Category Charts

- If you haven't done so while prereading before lecture, you can begin making a tentative chart during lecture.

- Wait until after you have gathered all the necessary information (been to lecture and read the text) on that topic before making the final version of your chart.

- How the syllabus, lecture and text are organized will give you ideas on how to organize your chart. For example, main headings and sub-headings.

- Use the charts in the text or handouts in addition to making your own.

- The maximum number for categories (either up and down or across) is five to seven. More than that becomes too much to quickly review.

- The first column (far left) on each chart should contain the name of the subject/topic/disease. The other columns will provide the details.

- You should be able to review each chart in five minutes or less. Repetition = Retention.

- When a lecturer makes a point of saying something that is not in your book, or if he or she disagrees with a portion of the text, put that in your chart!

- Some topics have information that doesn't fit your

chosen categories. When this happens it's a good idea to have "other" or "miscellaneous" as the last column to capture any important information that doesn't fit elsewhere on your chart.

- The information in the boxes of your chart is just a brief reminder. It should be very concise. It is only there to remind you of the complete information you have already studied and know.

- Make your charts visually attractive. If they look good, you'll be more likely to enjoy reviewing them, and you'll be more likely to remember the content.

- The text will usually organize information in a logical progression. You can lay out the columns in your chart according to that same sequence. (E.g., Etiology, Risk Factors, Pathophysiology, Clinical Manifestations, etc.)

- You can use Post-its™ to plan charts. If there are very many of them you can stick them on a wall or mirror and move them around until they are in a logical order.

- You can also use a whiteboard (dry erase board) to sketch out the categories as you plan your chart.

- Be forewarned! Creating a chart is often a messy process, involving trial-and-error, as you choose what information will be included. That's okay. It is the very process of choosing how to organize the information that begins to build a mental model which makes the chart (and the information) memorable.

- In the interest of saving time, students in study groups sometimes divide the job of creating charts among themselves. They then distribute copies of their charts with the other group members. If you choose to do this, double check for accuracy and plan to spend more time in review. Most students tell us they would rather make their own charts. The effort expended to organize the information makes it theirs. Students tell us it's the *act* of making the charts that increases comprehension and embeds the information in their memory.

- You WILL remember what is on your chart, so be sure that the information is accurate. It's hard to erase facts from your memory once they've been learned and repeated.

- Charts can be made either by hand or on the computer. If you develop a template you can print or copy it and use it repeatedly. (You can often begin to fill in a chart template during prereading, reading or lecture.)

Why Not Just Make Outlines?

Why don't we recommend outlining as one of our note-making methods?

- Outlines tend to become "loose notes," that is, disorganized. Though students may think they are outlining according to a hierarchical structure, often they abandon the formal outline and just end up with pages of unstructured information.

- Anything that can be outlined can be charted.

Charts, however, are vastly superior to outlines for learning, reviewing and self-testing. You'll be glad you took the time to make them.

Advantages of Charts Over Outlines

- The structure of a category chart organizes information in a highly memorable way.

- The similarities and differences among the details are the types of information that tend to appear on exams.

- Multiple choice questions are so easy to make from a chart that you might as well study the same information that way.

- A well-made chart is laid out so that the differences among the details inside the boxes are unmistakable.

- It's practically impossible to self-test from an outline, but is easy from a chart.

As an example, we have taken a student's outline on Hypoglycemia and Hyperglycemia (Chart 4.8) and turned it into a category chart (Chart 4.9). An interesting discovery we made, after we created the chart, was that there was information missing from the outline! No one had noticed that any information had been omitted until there were empty boxes in the category chart. That points up another advantage of category charts; an empty space in a category chart shows you that information is missing from your notes.

Outline of Hypoglycemia & Hyperglycemia

Hypoglycemia:
- Symptoms: *early*—fatigue, headache, drowsiness, tremulousness, nausea; *late*—sweating, nervousness, weakness, tremors, mental confusion, blurred vision
- Treatment:
  - ½ cup OJ
  - 5 crackers
  - 3 graham crackers
  - 6 oz milk
  - 6 Lifesavers
  - 15-20 g CHO
- or sticky fruit exchange (i.e., tsp honey or syrup)
- or Glucagon SC

Hyperglycemia:
- Symptoms: ↑ BS; excessive thirst, & urine output; drowsiness; red, dry skin; fruity breath odor; anorexia; abdominal pain, N / V; dry mouth; rapid, deep breathing; unconsciousness. DKA: pH ↓ 7.3; ↑ plasma ketone; BS > 300

Nursing Management:
- Assessment
  - —PE (skin, sensory, CV, GU, reproductive)
  - —Religion, diet, exercise
  - —Current drug use
  - —Support system
  - —Knowledge of disease / treatment
- Monitor
  - —Serum glucose / urine (serum > 180 will spill into urine, ketones, PRO)
  - —Hypoglycemia / hyperglycemia
  - —Skin, feet (brown spots are hemorrhages into skin)

Patient / Family Education:
- Hypoglycemia / hyperglycemia
- Sick day rules
  - —Notify Dr. if vomiting / diarrhea > 4 hr, < PO intake x 24 hr, illness > 24-48 h, > BS with PPP, ketones mod-large, progressive drowsiness; continue insulin, eat 50-100 g CHO q 10-15"
- Insulin—Preparation, administration, dosage, schedule, onset, peak, duration, care / storage, injection sites, no OTC
- Exercise—Benefits, after a meal, carry CHO, monitor BS before / after, wear ID, avoid exercise alone
- Nutrition—Schedule meals / snacks, how to plan meals, how to measure portions, eating out (refer to dietitian)
- Self-monitoring BS—Schedule for testing, testing procedure, storage of reagant strips, technique for cleaning monitor, method for recording.

Created by D. Griffith, The University of Texas Health Science Center — Houston

Chart 4.8

Outline on Hypoglycemia & Hyperglycemia Turned into a Category Chart

	Symptoms	Treatment	Nursing Management	Patient / Family Education
Hypoglycemia	*early*—fatigue, headache, drowsiness, tremulousness, nausea; *late*—sweating, nervousness, weakness, tremors, mental confusion, blurred vision	• 15-20g CHO • ½ cup OJ • 6 oz milk • 5 crackers • 6 Lifesavers • 3 graham crackers • or sticky fruit exchange (i.e., tsp honey or syrup) • or Glucagon SC		
Hyperglycemia	↑ BS; excessive thirst, & urine output; drowsiness; red, dry skin; fruity breath odor; anorexia; abdominal pain, N / V; dry mouth; rapid, deep breathing; unconsciousness. DKA: pH ↓ 7.3; ↑ plasma ketone; BS > 300		*Assessment* • PE (skin, sensory, CV, GU, reproductive) • Religion, diet, exercise • Current drug use • Support system • Knowledge of disease / treatment *Monitor* • Serum glucose / urine (serum > 180 will spill into urine, ketones, PRO) • Hypoglycemia / hyperglycemia • Skin, feet (brown spots are hemorrhages into skin)	*Sick day rules* Notify Dr. if vomiting / diarrhea > 4 hr, < PO intake x 24 hr, illness > 24-48 h, > BS with PPB ketones mod-large, progressive drowsiness; continue insulin, eat 50-100 g CHO q 10-15" *Insulin*—Preparation, administration, dosage; schedule, onset, peak, duration, care / storage, injection sites, no OTC *Exercise*—Benefits, after a meal, carry CHO, monitor BS before / after, wear ID, avoid exercise alone *Nutrition*—Schedule meals / snacks, how to plan meals, how to measure portions, eating out (refer to dietitian) *Self-monitoring BS*—Schedule for testing, testing procedure, storage of reagant strips, technique for cleaning monitor, method for recording.

Created by D. Griffith, The University of Texas Health Science Center — Houston, revised by K. Straker

Chart 4.9

How to Know When a Category Chart is the Best Type of Note for the Information

When the information to be remembered involves more than one category of sub-topic (e.g., three types of STDs) and more than one type of detail connected to each sub-topic (e.g., type of microorganism, method of transmission, symptoms, treatment, etc.) a category chart is recommended.

Below are some cue words that signal a category chart is probably your best choice:

- category
- compare
- contrast
- types of
- differences between or among
- similarities between or among
- factors. For example, discuss factors affecting...

Flow Charts

A flowchart shows the course, progression, or results of a process over time. If movement or change over time is involved, a flow chart is a good choice for your study note. Examples include: steps in a clinical plan; physiological processes (e.g., mechanisms of edema formation); steps in a disease process that depend on various types of treatments or lack of treatment (e.g., stages in diabetes and its treatment).

How do you create a flow chart? The first event or stage in the process is placed at the top or left of the page with an arrow leading to the second event or stage. In a flow chart the details are at the end of each arrow, and you may also box them for greater visual impact. Be imaginative! One student made jagged edges or "rays" to mark a detail that he thought was the most important one in the entire sequence. Color may also be very useful to point out differences or changes that occur.

Though most students draw their flow charts by hand, you may want to consider using software that will aid you in creating flow charts.

Advantages of Flow Charts	Disadvantages of Flow Charts
You can see the details in relation to each other and to the main topic.	Only useful for information that occurs in a temporal sequence.
The clear visual picture is memorable and easy to review.	
Easy to use for self-testing	
It's the only way to make a condensed note for some types of information.	

How to decide when to use a flow chart

Flow charts involve changes over time or a process. Below are some cue words that signal a flow chart might be your best choice:

- circulation
- cycle
- flow
- movement
- phases
- process
- sequence
- cascade
- progression

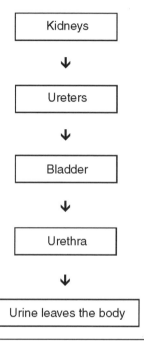

Sample Flowchart

Pathway of Urine Through the Urinary System

If your task was to learn the following process: urine is the fluid excreted by the kidneys, transported by the ureters to the urinary bladder where it is stored until it is voided through the urethra; you could create a simple flowchart to help you remember the order.

```
┌─────────────────────────┐
│         Kidneys         │
└─────────────────────────┘
            ↓
┌─────────────────────────┐
│         Ureters         │
└─────────────────────────┘
            ↓
┌─────────────────────────┐
│         Bladder         │
└─────────────────────────┘
            ↓
┌─────────────────────────┐
│         Urethra         │
└─────────────────────────┘
            ↓
┌─────────────────────────┐
│   Urine leaves the body │
└─────────────────────────┘
```

Created by K. Straker   Chart 4.10

Diagrams

Diagrams are the outlines or features of an object. They are probably the most common illustrations you will find in your textbooks.

A diagram is used when you are expected to know the name, location or the arrangement of parts of an object (usually an anatomical structure).

You can either copy diagrams from the text or related websites or draw them free hand. Here's where your artistic side can really shine! How you label the parts is the key to its usefulness for review and self test.

Labeling instructions:

1. The parts of the diagrams should be numbered (or lettered).

2. Draw a line from the numbered part out into the margin (a couple of inches, at least) where you will write the name of the numbered part.

3. You can cover the names in the margins when you self test.

Diagrams may not be the easiest type note from which to self test. Covering the labels with scrap paper, and writing on the paper what should be on the underlying label, make review and self-testing easier. Many students tell us that, as with the other structured note forms, it is the act of grappling with the information while creating the diagram that makes the information memorable.

Brain Diagram

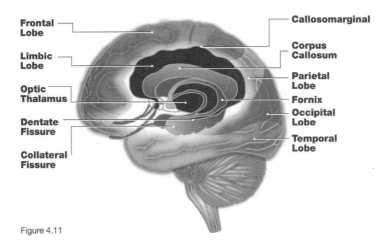

Frontal Lobe
Limbic Lobe
Optic Thalamus
Dentate Fissure
Collateral Fissure

Callosomarginal
Corpus Callosum
Parietal Lobe
Fornix
Occipital Lobe
Temporal Lobe

Figure 4.11

Advantages of Diagrams	Disadvantages of Diagrams
Visually interesting and generally easy to remember	Useful only for names and locations of structures.
Can be used to self-test if the names are placed to the side where they can be covered.	

Combined Note Forms

Combined note forms use elements of two or more of the previously-discussed kinds of notes.

For many topics you may find that combining note forms make sense. Students sometimes include a drawing on their vocabulary cards to help "jog" their memory. Another example is inserting a flow chart or diagram in a category chart, or perhaps using a note card for a very simple flow chart or category chart.

How might you complete the chart on the next two pages?

Digestion and Elimination
Combination Flow & Category — Partially Completed Chart

Mouth

Teeth	Saliva	Notes
Masticate (chew)	• Dilutes • Softens	Digestion begins in the mouth

Esophagus

Upper Esophageal Sphincter	Bolus of Food	Lower Esophageal (Cardiac) Sphincter	Notes
Circular muscle prevents air from entering the esophagus & food from refluxing into the throat.	Travels by peristalsis.	Not a muscle but a physiological pressure difference to prevent reflux.	

Stomach

3 Tasks	Produces & Secretes	Notes
Store Mix Empty	• HCI & pepsin (to facilitate protein digestion) • Mucus (to protect somach from acid & enzyme activity) • Intrinsic factor (essential in vitamin B12 absorption)	

Small Intestine

Movement by	Chyme	Duodenum	Jejunum	Ileum
Peristalsis Segmentation (these facilitate digestion & absorption)	Mixes w / digestive juices. Pastelike by the time it reaches end of small intestine.	2 ft. Continues to process chyme.	9 ft. Absorption of carbs & proteins.	12 ft. Absorption of water, fats & bile salts.

Created by K. Straker

Chart 4.12a

Continued

Vital Skills

Digestion and Elimination
Combination Flow & Category — Partially Completed Chart

Large Intestine

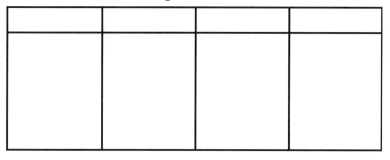

Anus

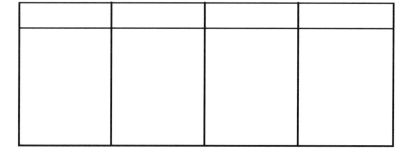

Defecation

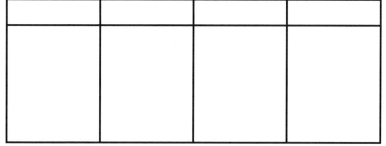

Created by K. Straker

Chart 4.12b

Mapping

Mapping is a pictorial tool used to arrange complex topics. Maps look a little like flow charts, but they are multi-factorial and multi-directional.

Maps are known by a variety of names: concept maps, networks, knowledge maps, semantic maps or process maps. They are typically used to deal with connections or relationships among concepts or themes and are, therefore, most often used at the highest level of generality. For example, they may be used as an introduction to a new topic or in summary of a recently discussed topic.

Both students and teachers have used them to summarize an entire course. Now that's seeing the big picture! But on objective exams you are not typically asked big picture or general questions. Nursing school exam questions usually focus on details, which are not easily learned by mapping. If you are asked to write an essay on a topic, however, a map could be useful. For example, a map could help you if you were asked to write down everything you know about diabetes.

Reference to the Decision Table ("How to Choose the Best Note-Making Format & Possible Cue Words" page 118) at the end of the chapter will help you decide how to choose the best type of note for your purpose. It summarizes the different styles of notes discussed in this chapter and, thus, nicely illustrates the usefulness of category charts. This Decision Table will help you to analyze the task first by asking yourself, "What kind of information is this?"

Advantages of Maps	Disadvantages of Maps
Useful to capture knowledge or summarize what is already known about a subject that is complex and covers a wide scope. (e.g., an entire course or textbook.)	Requires training in how to use.
Helpful in illustrating relationships across topics.	Maps don't provide the level of detail that appears in examinations.
Teacher-made maps can be used to introduce a topic or give an overview or summary of the course.	To include the necessary details, additional maps need to be created, which interferes with the goal of condensing the amount of information you have to learn.
	Lack the inherent structure to make the information memorable.
	The proponents of mapping, as well as the structure itself, discourage review and self-test.

CHAPTER 4

Help! I Can't Start Making My Notes Because I Don't Understand the Topic!

It's true that you must have some understanding before you can begin making your notes. The following chart will walk you through the steps to improve your comprehension of any topic.

Seven Steps to Better Understanding

1.	Go to the library.
2.	Find the shelf with textbooks on the subject you don't understand
3.	Choose 3-5 text books which cover the topic.
4.	Select recent editions, those with colorful illustrations, or one with an attractive, appealing layout.
5.	Sit down at a large table and open all the books to the specific topic you want to understand better.
6.	Read the explanation given in each of the books.
7.	Summarize what you find in some form of note.

Why does this work?

Every book explains the topic somewhat differently. Each author will take a slightly different tack, and one of these should "click" with you. The "ah-ha" may be an illustration or chart in the text, so make sure you look at those, too.

Some people hypothesize that looking at several texts works because of the repetitive nature and cumulative effect. Whatever the reason, it works! So give it a try next time you are feeling stuck.

You may also choose to use the internet and visit various sites to accomplish the same thing. That may work IF you can keep yourself focused on the task at hand and not become side-tracked by all the other interesting bits of information that you run across.

Scheduling Time to Make Good Notes

Your notes are central to the Vital Skills study system. Remember, **Success = System + Schedule**. You can't review and you can't self test without a good set of notes. It's important to take the time—whatever time it takes—to make a good set of notes. The act of creating the notes embeds the information in your brain. These notes will be used repeatedly to review for in-term exams, final course exams, clinical cases and licensing exams. They are worth the investment.

What's the Best Way to Store Your Notes for Easy Retrieval in the Future?

Type of Note	Storage
Note Cards	Long file boxes with tabs for each course and each major topic within the course. Small file boxes, like recipe boxes, for each course. Banded with rubber bands or on a ring.
Category Charts	File folders by course. Three-ring binders with tabs for each course and each major topic within the course.
Flow Charts	File folders by course. Three-ring binders with tabs for each course and each major topic within the course.
Diagrams	File folders by course. Three-ring binders with tabs for each course and each major topic within the course.
Combined Note Forms	File folders by course. Three-ring binders with tabs for each course and each major topic within the course.
Maps	File folders by course. Three-ring binders with tabs for each course and each major topic within the course.

 **Intervention**

Exercise — Reading and Note-Making

For the next week, schedule one to three hours a day each weekday and one long or two shorter study periods on the weekend. This will be your main study activity outside of lecture. Make as many different notes as the material permits including note cards, category charts, flow charts, diagrams or combined charts.

How much time is required to study for each course will depend on the density of the information and your prior familiarity with the topic, but one to two hours of personal study per classroom hour continues to be a reasonable guideline. The goal of note-making is to free yourself from the text and other assigned materials. Your final set of study notes should include everything you absolutely want to know. You will get faster with practice and will learn to make mental notes as new information is encountered.

You will start to think in a different way and will:

- notice how the information is organized,
- be more alert to what information is important,
- be vigilant about what details support the main idea.

Some educators call this "critical thinking." You might also think of it as "careful thinking." In the learning process, critical thinking begins with prereading. Here is a simple flowchart to illustrate the point:

The Critical Thinking Process
Used in Making Notes

— Preread from text, syllabus, handouts —
Think about the type of notes that
would be best for the material.

— Attend lecture —
Begin making tentative charts or notes during lecture.

— Read the text —

— Decide how to arrange the final charts or notes —
Make notes. Include information from course
objectives, syllabus, handouts and other sources.

*A note to students who have class quizzes over the reading material. In this case we recommend that you preread and read the text **before** attending the lecture. The "pop" quizzes are typically intended as an incentive to read the text prior to lecture.*

Creating an Environment Conducive to Study

If you find you are having difficulty studying because of noise or visual distractions, skip ahead to Chapter 6 and implement some of the strategies that will help you create a good study environment. Improved concentration increases what you remember and can often decrease the length of your study periods!

After one week of note-making, complete the Check-up exercise below. You may continue with the next chapter on Review and Self-test during that time.

 **Evaluation**

Check-Up on the Reading and Note-Making Exercise

1. Did you understand the material better after you made the notes? If so, why?

   _____

   _____

2. List the different types of notes you made for each class.

   _____

   _____

3. What difficulties, if any, did you encounter?

   _____

   _____

4. How did this process begin to change the way you think about the information?

   _____

   _____

 **Summary**

Note-making is the heart and soul of this study system.

Success = System + Schedule

Good notes:

- Increase comprehension. You can't make a good set of notes without understanding the material.

- Save time. You have only one thing (your set of notes) to review.

- Focus your attention on what you need to know by combining and condensing information from multiple sources.

- Help you become a critical thinker. You can distinguish what is truly important in the midst of much detailed information.

How to Choose the Best
Note-Making Format & Possible Cue Words

If the Task is to:	And the Information is:	Make this Type of Note	Examples	Possible Cue Words
Recall unrelated, specific information (e.g., definitions or formulae); very small charts; or details from larger charts that you still need to learn	Not complicated enough to require a full 8½ x 11 sheet of paper	Note Cards	Any class	• Abbreviations • Define (vocabulary words) • Forgotten details • Formulae • Short lists
Compare / contrast or classify a set of main topics according to a set of similar details	Static / unchanging	Category Chart	Pathology, Pharmacology, Med-Surg. (any disease)	• Category • Compare • Contrast • Describe • Difference between / among • Discuss factors
Associate a name with a location	Static / unchanging & related information is due only to location	Diagram	Anatomy, Assessment	• Locate • Name structure • Position
Associate a complicated series of names, procedures or functions	Changing in a temporal chronological sequence or cause / effect sequence	Flow Chart	Physiology, Parasitic lifecycles, (any process or cycle)	• Circulation • Cycle • Flow • Movement • Phases • Process • Sequence
Associate complicated but related set of information involving names, location / details of function	Static / unchanging	Combine Diagram w / Category Chart	Any class	
Compare / contrast & see contacts between more than one complicated, but related, process	Changing in a temporal / chronological sequence	Combine Flow Chart by Categories	Any class	
To get the "big picture" of a topic at a highly conceptual level	Irregular, complex associations—including cause / effect	Concept Map	Overview, across disciplines, whole systems	

Table 4.1

Student Feedback

I made note cards, flow charts and category charts. Making the notes helped me understand how to approach the material.

I made note cards and category charts for Health Assessment and Pathophysiology. They helped me break down the information into main ideas and details. That way I got the big picture and all the details.

I made note cards, category charts and flow charts. Writing something down really makes it stick in my head better than just reading it.

The act of putting it together required me to focus more. It really helps to create a 'blueprint.'

Making charts really helped me to concentrate my study materials into an amount I could review for the test.

I used to waste study time not learning while reading. Now it takes less time to learn more, because I condense what I've studied into charts.

Some of my charts are so useful that I've condensed them further and carry them with me during clinicals.

It took a while to make a good set of notes, but, once I did, I knew the information! It was great!

It puts the information in perspective and helps the details jump out at you.

It takes more time to make these types of notes. But once you've made them, you KNOW the material.

I've realized that when you make your own set of notes, the information stays with you and you understand it better. It is not a waste of time—like when you're just reading it and not getting it.

References

Annis, L.F. & Davis, K.J. (1977). Study technique and cognitive style: Their effect on recall and recognition. *Journal of Educational Research*, 71, 175-178.

> Study indicates underlining while reading leads to greater understanding than reading alone, but writing notes while reading is significantly better for retention than reading and highlighting.

Bretzing, B.H. & Kulhavey, R.W. (1979). Note-taking and depth of processing. *Contemporary Educational Psychology*, 4 (2), 145-153.

> Students who take notes on reading assignments perform better on exams and the more organized their notes, the greater their comprehension and recall.

Brown, A.L., Compione, J.C. & Day, J.D. (1981). Learning to learn: On training students to learn from texts. *Educational Researcher*, 10, 14-21.

> Describes the possible relationships among different types of information to be learned and the effect on learning of incorporating those relationships into notes.

Bruner, J.S. (1961). The act of discovery. *Harvard Educational Review*, 31, 21-32.

> The importance of organizers in remembering and recalling information. The act of making your own notes or organizers is a big part of the learning process.

Clark, R. C. & Lyons, C. (2004). *Graphics for learning*. San Francisco: Pfeiffer, 133-138.

> Studies show that using charts (matrices) to study information increases retention by 10-20% over reading the text or studying an outline.

Edmondson, K.M. (1994). Concept maps and the development of cases for problem-based learning. *Academic Medicine*, 69, 108-110.

> Concept maps are often associated with problem-based learning because they encourage students to cross topic boundaries/ disciplines to find relationships among information.

Foshay, W.R., Silber, K.H. & Stelnicki, M.B. (2003) Writing training materials that work. San Francisco: Jossey-Bass/Pfeiffer.

A guide based on current cognitive psychology and instructional design theory and research. This book addresses creating instructional materials, which is what students do when they create study notes for their own learning.

Hoefler, P.A. (2003). *Successful problem-solving & test-taking for beginning nursing students*, Burtonsville, MD: MEDS Publishing.

This book is not just for beginning nursing students. It has many examples for students to work through as they learn to decipher what the question is "really" asking. It also includes a CD-ROM.

Holley, C.D. & Dansereau, D.F. (1984). Networking: The technique and the empirical evidence. *Spatial learning strategies: Techniques, applications and related issues*. New York: Academic Press, 81-108.

Describes the mapping strategy, called "networking", developed at Texas Christian University and discusses the theoretical basis for this strategy.

Isaacs, G. (1989). Lecture note-taking, learning and recall. *Medical Teacher*, 11: 295-302.

Review of literature on student note-taking and the extent to which they actually learn as a direct or indirect result of taking notes.

Lambiotte, J.G., Dansereau, D.F., Cross, D.R., & Reynolds, S.B. (1989). Multirelational semantic maps. *Educational Psychology Review*, 1, 331-367.

Describes features of knowledge maps, and considers both their strengths and weaknesses.

Novak, J.D. & Gowin, D.B. (1984). *Concept mapping for meaningful learning: Learning how to learn*. New York: Cambridge University Press.

This is the book that introduced concept mapping to medical educators. The authors discourage the memorization of maps.

Peper, R.J., & Mayer, R.E. (1978). Note-taking as a generative activity. *Journal of Educational Psychology*, 70 (4), 514-522.

Outlines three possible explanations for why the overt activity of note-making affects the learning outcome: 1) increases overall attention and orientation to new material; 2) requires more effort and deeper encoding of the material than does merely reading; 3) requires organizing and "making sense" of the material, which tends to integrate new material to information acquired previously.

Pinto, A.J. & Zeitz, H.J. (1997). Concept mapping: a strategy for promoting meaningful learning in medical education. *Medical Teacher*, 19 (2), 114-121.

Proposes training in concept mapping to enhance learning.

Quirk, M.E. (1994). *How to learn and teach in medical school.* Springfield, MA: Charles C. Thomas.

Though memorization is currently somewhat devalued in medical education, particularly in problem-based curricula, memory and thinking are inextricably linked. Memorized facts need to be placed in larger context to be readily generalized to a variety of applications.

Riegelman, R.K., & Hirsch, R.P. (1996). *Studying a study and testing a test: How to read the health science literature.* Boston: Little, Brown and Company.

A practical, but very detailed, guide for effective reading of health literature.

Russell, I.J., Caris, T.N., Harris, G.D., & Hendricson, W.D. (1983). Effects of three types of lecture notes on medical student achievement. *Journal of Medical Education*, 58, 627-636.

Study showed medical students who made their own notes from lectures had better retention of lecture information than students who received detailed handouts for the same lectures and did not need to create their own notes. Conclusion: Making notes imbeds information in memory.

Shimmerlik, S.M., & Nolan, J.D. (1976). Reorganization and recall of prose. *Journal of Educational Psychology*, 68 (6), 779-786.

Reorganization of material leads to improved academic performance on free recall tests.

Willey, M.S., & Jarecky, B.M. (1976). *Analysis and application of information.* Unpublished manuscript, Howard University, College of Medicine, Washington, D.C.

Using outlines and charts to commit information to memory.

CHAPTER 4

Review and Self-Test

(Week 3)

I feel more confident when I review and test myself.

✓ Assessment: How Do You Review and Self-Test?

Never Rarely Sometimes Often Always		

Directions: Mark the number that describes your current system of review and self-test.

4 (3) 2 1 0   1. I don't have time to review all the material before a test.

4 3 (2) 1 0   2. I concentrate on getting the "big picture" rather than the details.

0 1 2 3 (4)   3. I test myself over my notes to make sure I remember the material.

0 1 2 3 (4)   4. I review the material at least once a week while preparing for the next exam.

0 1 (2) 3 4   5. I schedule some time every day for review.

0 1 2 (3) 4   6. My notes are very organized, which allows me to frequently review the material before an exam.

0 1 2 3 4   7. The way I study identifies details that I
don't remember so I can spend more
time on them.

0 1 2 3 4   8. I schedule enough time to make at least
two or three reviews of the material
before a test.

4 3 2 1 0   9. Until I take an exam I don't know how
well prepared I am. The classroom exam
is the first time I've been tested over the
material.

0 1 2 3 4   10. When I get tired of reading and note-
making, I switch to reviewing or self-
testing.

_____   **Total Score** *(Add all the numbers that you circled.)*

Feedback on Review and Self-Test Answers

1. A good note format (highly organized and condensed) will streamline the review process so you
will have time for several reviews before a test.

2. How often are you asked about the "big picture"
on a multiple-choice exam? The multiple choice
format requires knowledge of details and the
differences among them. You need to place the
details in context. By just reading, you get the big
picture. It's making the notes and reviewing that
put the detail into your memory.

3. Good! And we hope your notes are designed to

make it easy to test yourself. Self-testing shows you what information needs more review.

4. Repetition is the key to memory. All research on memory shows that repeated review is the best way to remember anything.

5. Not only repeated reviews, but spaced intervals between reviews are important. Schedule time for review every day.

6. Excellent! An organized format allows frequent reviews and self-test.

7. You are saving time by focusing on what you've not yet mastered!

8. Give yourself a pat on the back. Repetition is the key to memory!

9. Don't wait! *Before* the exam is the time to find out what you don't know. By *self*-testing, prior to the exam, you will know what material needs further review.

10. Excellent idea. Varying study activities can help you study for longer periods of time.

Score Interpretation — Review and Self-Test

34-40   Very good!
27-33   Good, but could use improvement
Below 27   Help is on the way! Read this chapter carefully.

Goal: Repeated Reviews

You've gone to a lot of trouble to make those fabulous notes. The process of making them begins to embed the information in your brain—but it's the repeated reviews that will solidify the information and make it memorable for the long term. Information must be stored in long-term memory before it can be easily accessed and applied—and you know how your instructors love to ask questions which require you to apply the information you have learned!

Remember — Repetition is the key to memory

 # Rationale

Scientific research consistently finds that spaced practice improves memory. The number of repetitions and the time in between those repetitions are two main factors involved in the recall of information. For example, if you wanted to learn the twelve cranial nerves, it would be a mistake to go over each one 20 times in one sitting and think you had reviewed enough. You'd remember more if you only reviewed each card or chart twice per sitting at five spaced intervals during the day. It is only half the number of repetitions, but you'll be more likely to remember the information.

In nursing school, you will typically have two to three weeks between course exams. In that short time, how will you be able to review repeatedly? This brief time frame makes it imperative that you stay caught up on your notes. There is no leeway.

If you are reviewing properly you will be eliminating material (by putting it into your "know" pile), which will enable you to focus your time on the material that needs more review (your "don't know" pile). Students often believe that recently presented course material is still "fresh" in their minds, when actually it is easier to forget because they have had fewer opportunities to review it.

"Review is how you get the information to stick."

How many reviews can you fit into the brief period between tests? Ideally, you will be reviewing every day, sorting your notes into "know" and "don't know" piles and continually adding your new notes as you make them. Just before the exam you will want to review and self-test all your notes, including those from the "know" pile, to be sure you have retained the information. By test time you should have had at least two reviews of all of the material and at least one self-test. You will have encountered portions of the material eight or nine times:

1. Prereading
2. Lecture
3. Rough lecture notes
4. Reading

5. Final set of notes
6. Spaced review
7. Spaced review
8. Self-test
9. Final review of everything before the exam.

How could you NOT know the information using this system?

Three Reasons to Self-Test

1. Be prepared. Rather than being surprised on test day, why not test yourself in advance, while you still have time to remediate? Tests tell the teacher how well you have mastered the material, but why wait? You can walk into a test confident that your preparation was thorough.

2. Save time. Your self-tests will tell you where you need to spend your time. Material that you have mastered will be set aside until the final review—a day or two prior to the exam.

3. Self-testing wakes you up, increases your motivation and focuses your attention. Once you realize you don't know an item, you will be ready to take action!

Although it feels good to review material that you have mastered, it's to your benefit to pay more attention to what you don't know, and spend your time in review of the less familiar material.

Sources for Self-Testing

In addition to using your own notes for self testing, many faculty members also encourage students to use NCLEX-type questions from review books. This has the added advantage of helping students become familiar with the way standardized exam questions are worded, which is sometimes different from how your instructor might phrase the same item.

How to Review and Self Test

Quickly read the information on a chart one or two times. Immediately cover the entire chart except for the outside labels across the top and down the far left column. Write or say the answers to test yourself to see how much of it you remember. That's all there is to it. You should consider the content mastered when you score a 90% or higher on the entire chart. The rule for effective reviewing is to do it quickly and frequently.

Taking time to write the answers has two main benefits. 1) It will keep you honest. Once you commit your answer to paper, it is much more difficult to say, "That's what I meant," when you look at the answer and discover that what you have written doesn't match what is in the chart. If that happens, then you have not yet mastered the information. 2) Writing the answer has a kinesthetic benefit. The act of writing helps embed information in your long-term memory.

Tips for Reviewing and Self-Testing

- Carry 10 to 20 note cards with you each day.

- Select a corner of your chart to keep track of reviews (R) and self-tests (ST) by making tally marks on the charts or diagrams themselves. For example R// means you have reviewed that chart twice and ST 70% means you have self-tested once and scored 70%, which means you have not yet mastered the material. Mastery is 90% or better.

- Each box in a category chart can be thought of like a note card. If you miss only a few boxed items you can pencil in a small check mark (v) in that box to remind you that item needs further review. If, after two or three reviews, you have not learned those details, then make note cards for those facts. You can also make note cards for details you have not learned from flow charts or diagrams.

- Carrying charts in file folders labeled "know" and "don't know" or in a binder with tabs labeled "know" and "don't know" also makes them portable. Students often carry the binder or folders instead of a text when they know they'll have time during the day to review.

- To self-test you can use a white board to sketch out the chart or diagram.

- Keep your review periods short. We suggest no more than five minutes per chart or diagram. This will ensure sufficient time for repeated reviews at spaced intervals.

When to Schedule Your Review and Self-Test Time

If you are an early riser, do your review first thing in the morning. If you're not, just before dinner is often a good time to schedule a session for review and self-test. The weekend also works well, because you are not getting new information during that time.

You should plan to spend twenty to thirty minutes

per day on reviewing and self-testing. You will spend more time reviewing as the exam approaches, of course. But you will not be in "frantic cramming mode," because you will know you have done a good job of preparing.

Some students find that taping copies of their charts on the bathroom mirror or bedroom closet door can help them use odd bits of time (while brushing teeth, fixing hair, or getting dressed) to review important material.

Study Tip: Sleepiness or fatigue during a study period may be a cue that it's time to switch activities. Self-testing will often raise your level of motivation, especially when you find out you don't know some of the material.

Scoring Self-Tests

In order to know how well you have mastered the material, we suggest that you score the self-tests. For example, if you are reviewing a category chart that has five columns and five rows, you will have 25 details to master. When you self-test and miss ten of those items, you may say to yourself, "I knew most of the information." That is correct. You knew 15 out of 25 items. But "most" of the information (15/25) is only 60%. That score is not high enough to pass an exam. You should plan to master 90% of the information that you have in your notes.

Why 90%? Tests are a sample of the content assigned. Your notes probably will not cover 100% of the content. To increase the odds that your sample of the material matches what the teacher samples on the exam, near complete mastery of your notes will increase your odds of doing well. The ratio of the two samples is not 1:1, so you need to get a higher percentage of correct answers on your own notes to ensure you do well on the exam.

✓ Interventions

Three Exercises to Incorporate Reviewing and Self-Testing into Your Schedule

Exercise 1

You should already have a regular schedule of prereading, reading and note-making. Now add twenty to thirty minutes a day for review and self-test for the next week.

Exercise 2

Carry 10-20 note cards with you and review them at least four or five times each day. When you sort them in the evening you should be able to put most of them into your "know" pile.

Exercise 3

After you have reviewed your charts, self test. Keep track of your score next to the ST written on your chart. For example, ST/ (60%), / (75%), / (90%).

At the end of the week return to the Evaluation section and complete the Check-Up.

 **Evaluation**

Check-Up: Exercises to Incorporate Reviewing and Self-Testing into Your Schedule

1. Did you schedule a time for review and self-test every day? What time of day worked best for you?

   _____

   _____

2. Did you carry and sort 10-20 note cards every day? If so, how many reviews did you average?

   _____

   _____

3. What percentage of the note cards went into the "know" pile each day?

   _____

   _____

4. About how many charts did you review each day? What percentage of mastery did you typically achieve when you self-tested?

   _____

   _____

 **Summary**

Success = System + Schedule

Congratulations! You have completed the portion of the book that teaches the heart of this study skills system.

It began with time management. Through the experiences provided by the time planning and management exercises, you have learned to schedule enough time for the study system that followed.

The components of the Vital Skills Study System are:

- Prereading,
- Reading and Note Making,
- Reviewing and Self-Testing.

This study system focuses on learning details and storing information in long-term memory. Information must be stored in long-term memory before it can be applied in a meaningful way.

Coming Up Next

In the next four chapters (Keeping Focused, Productive Self-Talk, Test Taking and NCLEX Preparation) we will cover important ways you can enhance this study system. You can achieve even greater success by reading the chapters and implementing these additional strategies.

Vital Skills Study Strategies — Quick Overview

Type of Study Activity	Approximate % of Time	Time of Day / Week	Purpose / Rationale	Study Behavior
Prereading	5-10%	Immediately prior to lecture or the evening before lecture.	Advance organizer. See the big picture of the topic to be covered in lecture. Increase concentration during lecture. Improve lecture notes.	Use book, syllabus or PowerPoint. Look for objectives; summary; bold-faced words; charts; diagrams; study questions. Ask yourself, "What is this page about?" or "What main topic is covered in this section / chapter / slide?"
Reading and Note-making	60-70%	After lecture. Choose best time of day for high concentration. Schedule 2+ hours consecutively if possible.	Fit details into the big picture. Understand how to apply principles, if appropriate.	Undistracted concentration until you have a clear understanding of principles or of details and main topic. Make charts. Make diagrams. Make cards.
			Organize into easily memorable format, if a memory task. Make organized and compact notes for review and self-test.	
Reviewing	15-25%	Either first or last study activity—daily.	Increase retention, speed and recall.	Re-read charts, diagrams, cards—any condensed notes.
Self-Testing	5-10%	After review. When motivation drops during a study period or as a change from other study activities. At least weekly.	Increase motivation. Check on retention. Aid to planning further review of specific topics.	Sort flash cards. Cover details in charts and fill in details on another sheet of paper. Ask yourself questions and score the answers. Sort into "know" and "don't know" stacks. Continue to review "don't knows" until you reach 90% comprehension.

Table 5.1

Student Feedback

It is so much easier to review using my own notes. I used to try and review from the book, but there was just too much information.

I am now prepared, focused and confident!

Before I learned this study system I procrastinated and found it hard to study more than an hour or two. Now it's not hard for me to get started, and I can go on—with regular 10 to 15 minute breaks—for up to 5 or 6 hours!

I have my time planned out, I preread, take notes and self test. These strategies are really helping me to study better and know the material well.

When I review and self test I can spend more time on what I don't know. It really saves time.

Now that I self test, I know what I need to spend more time studying.

Tests aren't so scary when I've already self-tested. I know that I know the material!

 # References

Clark, R.C. & Lyons, C. (2004). *Graphics for learning*. San Francisco: Pfeiffer.

> Explores the way graphics support the learning process. Research regarding cognitive load, building mental models or schema and the use of matrices or charts is especially pertinent.

Corkill, A.J., Glover, J.A., Bruning, R.H. & Krug, D. (1988). Advance organizers: Retrieval context hypotheses. *Journal of Educational Psychology*, 80, 3: 304-311.

> Rereading notes had a significant effect on recall.

Farr, M.J. (1987). *The long-term retention of knowledge and skills.* New York: Springer-Verlag.

A thorough review of the scientific literature on learning, memory and retention, including Ebbinghaus' work originally published in 1885.

Jacobson, R.L. (1986, September 3). Memory experts' advice: Forget about that string around your finger. *The Chronicle of Higher Education*, 49.

Survey of psychologists involved in memory research stated that their personal preference was for writing things down in order to remember them. They also recommend organizing and repeating information. They do not recommend the use of mnemonic devices for most practical applications.

Howard, P.J., (2000). *The owner's manual for the brain: Everyday applications from mind-brain research* (2nd ed.). Atlanta, GA: Bard Press.

Chapter 7 is entitled A Good Night's Sleep: Cycles, Drams, Naps and Nightmares and reviews research of each, including the link between sleep and memory.

Novak J.D. & Gowin, D.B. (1984). *Concept mapping for meaningful learning, Learning how to learn.* New York: Cambridge University Press.

This is the book that introduced the concept of mapping to medical educators. The authors discourage the memorization of maps.

Sisson, J.C., Swartz, R.D., & Wolf, F.M. (1992). Learning, retention and recall of clinical information. *Medical Education*, 26:454-461.

Students lost between 10 and 20 percent comprehension when taking the same test 90 days later with no review.

Spitzer, H.F. (1939). Studies in retention. *Journal of Educational Psychology*, 30: 641-656.

Study shows much greater retention, even 60 days after reading, if material is reviewed. Believes that review should occupy up to 90% of study time.

CHAPTER 5

Keeping Focused

(Week 4)

> *Increasing my concentration helps me get a lot more out*
> *of my study time. It doesn't take as long to figure things*
> *out when I'm really focused.*

 ## Assessment: Factors Affecting Concentration

Directions: The following 21 statements describe a particular study
situation. Indicate how much (or how frequently) each statement
applies to your own study style, according to the following scale:

1 = seldom (less than 20 % of the time)
2 = sometimes (21-40% of the time)
3 = often (41-60% of the time)
4 = usually (61-80% of the time)
5 = almost always (81-100% of the time)

Circle the number that best reflects your current
study habits.

1 2 3 ④ 5   1. As I read and take notes, I tell myself that I am interested in the information.

1 2 3 4 ⑤   2. I sit at a desk while studying.

1 2 3 4 ⑤   3. I study in a quiet place.

Seldom	Sometimes	Often	Usually	Almost Always		

① 2 3 4 5   4. I am able to study for two hours without taking a break.

1 2 **③** 4 5   5. I am alert and focused while studying.

1 2 3 4 **⑤**   6. I avoid distractions, such as music or TV while studying.

1 2 3 4 **⑤**   7. I set a goal for the amount of work I want to get done in each study period.

1 2 3 4 **⑤**   8. If I begin to feel tired during a study period, I take a brief break to eat a snack or do some quick exercises to boost my energy in order to get back into my studies with renewed concentration.

1 2 **③** 4 5   9. I do not stare out the window or day dream during a study period.

1 2 **③** 4 5   10. I deliberately keep a slight sense of urgency or time pressure while studying.

1 2 3 4 **⑤**   11. My study space is cleared of everything other than the materials I need to study at that time.

1 2 3 4 **⑤**   12. As I study, I think about how I can use this information when I am a nurse.

① 2 3 4 5   13. During a reading session, I set a goal for how fast to read each page.

1 2 **③** 4 5   14. I do not doze off or feel sleepy during a study session.

CHAPTER 6

         Vital Skills

1 ②3 4 5   15. I do not usually think about doing some thing else (dates with friends, things I need to do, things I'd rather do, etc.) during a study session.

1 ②3 4 5   16. If I catch my thoughts wandering while studying, I immediately stop those thoughts and return my attention to my work.

1 2 3 4 ⑤   17. I routinely study at the same place and at regular times.

1 2 3 ④5   18. I don't study while lying down on a sofa or bed.

①2 3 4 5   19. Once I start studying, I do not need to take frequent breaks from my work.

1 2 ③4 5   20. As I study, I think how useful the information will be to me in the future.

1 2 ③4 5   21. I jump right into my work as I start my study session.

13

Score Interpretation — Factors Affecting Concentration

There are seven concentration factors to score. It will be important for you to know which, if any, of these factors may be a problem for you. There are three questions for each of the seven factors. Your score for each factor will be the sum of the numbers you circled for each of these three questions. Since the scale is 1-5, with 5 as the highest possible for each question, the maximum possible score for

CHAPTER 6

each factor is 15 (3 x 5). You can calculate your percentage on each factor by dividing 15 into your score.

Example			
Factor	My Factor Score	Total Possible	My %
Being awake and alert while studying Items 2, 5, 14	3 + 2 + 3 = 8	15	53% (8/15)
	(sum of scores on on the three questions)		(53% effective on this factor)

Use the form on page 143 to record your calculations from the Assessment.

Now you can calculate your score on each of the seven concentration factors and also your overall concentration score.

7 Factors	My Factor Score	My % ÷ by 15
1. Questions about being **awake & alert** during study sessions. Add scores for items 2, 5, 14	12 11	90 73 %
2. Questions about maintaining a **positive mood** while studying. Add scores on items 1, 12, 20	13 12	86.7 80 %
3. Questions about avoiding **external distractions**. Add scores on items 3, 6, 11	14 15	93.3 100 %
4. Questions about avoiding **internal distractions** (that distract you from your studies). Add scores on items 9, 15, 16	13 7	86.7 46 %
5. Questions about maintaining a sense of urgency while studying by **working fast**. Sum of scores on items 7, 10, 12	13 13	86.7 86 %
6. Questions about ability to **study for relatively long periods** of time without stopping. Sum of items 4, 8, 19	10 7	66.7 46 %
7. Questions about **cues in the study environment** that prompt you to start studying. Items 17, 18, 21	10 12	66.7 80 %
Overall concentration score. Sum of All Factor Scores above.	84 77	Overall Score
Overall concentration percentage. Sum of All Factor Scores divided by 105	80.9 73	Overall %

CHAPTER 6

The most important question of all is, "Are you getting the most out of your study time?"

Look at the "My Percentage" columns on page 143. Circle the three *lowest* percentages. These are the areas that present the most opportunity for improvement.

If your percentage for each factor was consistently at 80% or better, hurray! You are focused on your work when you study.

The scores which you circled are the factors to which you should pay most attention in the rest of the chapter.

Concentrating on your work is a skill that can be learned, just like any other skill.

If your overall score was lower that 60%, you will reap benefits from reading this chapter carefully and doing all the exercises faithfully. Remember, this is a **workbook**. Doing the exercises is what will help you improve.

Goal: Accomplish More in Less Time

What would you say if someone offered you six extra hours of study time every week? Would you believe it was possible? If you scored lower than 60% on any concentration factor, we believe you can give yourself that gift of time.

Let's do the calculation. Suppose you spend 20 hours a week in personal study (studying on your own, not in class). If you are concentrating only 50% of that time, you are wasting at least ten whole hours every week! If you can raise your level of concentration even ten percent, you can gain two more hours. If you can get your level of concentration up to 80%, you will recapture six whole hours each and every week. Over a 15-week semester, that would add up to 90 additional hours of study! Think how much extra review you could gain with that 90 extra hours to study! Or, seen the other way, wouldn't it be great to have that many hours freed up for other activities, because you were more efficient in your work?

Rationale and Interventions

Seven Factors Affecting Concentration

Factor 1 — Awake and Alert

When you feel wide awake and vigilant for important information, you obviously can learn more in less time. If you are sleepy, or hungry, or restless, it's hard to concentrate on any task. Taking care to have adequate sleep, nutrition, and exercise are the first steps to efficient study. You need at least seven hours of sleep on week nights, with some extra sleep on weekends. You need to eat three meals and a maybe a couple of snacks a day and get some regular exercise. When you study, put your work in the center of your desk or study table, directly under a good light. Your posture should be telling you that you are awake and alert. Sit straight up in a back-supporting chair. Do not recline in an armchair or on a bed or sofa. Lying down suggests to your body (and your brain) that it is time for rest or sleep. Keep your spine straight, your feet flat on the floor, your eyes on your study materials, and your hands ready to turn pages or make notes. Your posture tells you that you are ready to work.

"She has forgotten that increased concentration
means less study time!"

Exercise 1

Set a timer for ten minute intervals. Whenever the beeper sounds, check your posture. Is your back straight? Are your eyes directly over your study materials? Are your feet flat on the floor? Keep doing this exercise until your body is always in the awake and alert position when you are studying.

Exercise 2

To maintain your energy during a long study period, prepare in advance easy-to-eat snacks, such as vegetable sticks, crackers, nuts, cheese, or fruits. These snacks don't take much time to prepare, and they will keep up your energy while you study. Don't take more than ten minutes to consume your snacks during an hour of study. Recall from Chapter 2 that you must study at least 50 minutes of every hour to count an hour of study.

Exercise 3

When you notice that your attention begins to lag, switch study activities. You can do some prereading for the next day's lecture. Or, to really rouse yourself from lethargy, start to self-test over material you previously studied. Self-testing is highly motivating, especially if you find you can't remember some important information. A little anxiety can be a big wake-up call. Use your notes and charts for self-testing. When you change strategies, put aside whatever you were doing when you got sleepy and completely switch to another study activity.

Exercise 4

If you're feeling drowsy, take a ten-minute break for physical exercise to pump your blood up to your brain. You don't need a gym or special equipment to do toe touches, push-ups, jumping jacks, deep knee bends, or stretching exercises. Turn on some music and dance! Again, no more than ten minutes before you're back at work with more oxygen in your brain.

Vital Skills

Factor 2 — Positive Attitude

Encourage yourself. It's hard to work well when you don't feel good about what you're doing. Imagine two tennis players. One has to run cross-court to hit a speeding ball. He is thinking, "It's too far. I'll never make it." The other player must run from the back baseline to the net to hit a dropped ball. She thinks "Run for it! You can do it!" Which player is more likely to reach the ball on time? This is not to say you can think yourself into doing anything you want to do, but thinking you *can't* do something, or *don't like* to do something, or *don't want* to do something, will certainly not help you succeed at that something.

If you're thinking, "I can't control what I think (or how I feel)," think again! You can control your mood by controlling what you think. Emotions are the result of thoughts, and you are, or should be, in charge of your own thoughts. In our example about running for a ball, you can improve your chances of getting there if you think, "I can get it!" Or at least, "Go for it!" Read Chapter 7 about productive self-talk very carefully.

Here are some examples of internal messages (thoughts, feelings) that **get in the way** of productive studying:

> *I wish I could go out with my friends tonight instead of studying.*
> *I'll never get all this information into my head.*
> *I'll never need to know all this stuff anyway.*

And, here are some examples of internal messages that **help** you stay focused on your studies:

> *This information is interesting.*
> *This information will be useful to me, not only on the test next week but in the future*

when I am a nurse.
I really want to be an RN. I am fortunate to
be able to work toward my goal.
I'll feel good when I have learned this
information.

Here are three suggestions for productive thinking when studying. Tell yourself your studies are:

- **Interesting**. If you really want to be a nurse, what you are learning *should* be interesting, because you will need to know it to do your job properly.

- **Useful**. Say to yourself, "I need to know this in order to be a good nurse." Think as you begin your study session, "I'll need to know this someday soon." You can also think to yourself, "Knowing this information may help me save a person's life."

- Helping you **achieve your goal**. To achieve your goal, you need to pass each class and pass the NCLEX. Try to conjure up a mental picture of yourself using the information in a clinical setting.

Exercise 1

Have you ever noticed how championship divers take a moment to "psych up" just as they are about to execute a dive? They are mentally preparing themselves by envisioning successfully completing their dive. Before each study session during the next week, take a moment to say something motivating about learning the material you have scheduled to study. By "psyching up" at the beginning of each study session, you put yourself in a good frame of mind to concentrate and learn.

Here are some suggestions for motivating thoughts as you start your study session:

I really want to learn all I can about this topic.
This topic is really interesting.
This topic is really important.
I really want to concentrate all my energy on
learning this topic.
My thoughts will be only on the information I
am studying.

Factor 3 — External Distractions

In the chapter on time management, we suggested that sometimes you can save time by doing two things at once. This suggestion does not apply to studying. Don't try to do something else while studying.

To improve your concentration, turn off all background noise. Students often claim that having background music helps them study. Ask yourself, "If I am listening to the music at any level at all, is not some part of my brain distracted away from my studies?" Whether it is the television, radio, CD or iTunes, some part of your brain is paying attention to it. In fact, recent research indicates that multitasking slows you down and increases the chance of making a mistake in your work. It seems the lateral frontal and prefrontal cortex and possibly the superior frontal cortex cannot process two tasks at once. So turn off the TV, your iPod or MP3 player. The single exception to this rule is for those diagnosed with ADHD; some studies indicate that they may benefit from listening to music while they study.

Your study area itself may be distracting. Do not place your study desk or table near a window where you can see what is going on outdoors. You do not want a view to pull your eyes away from your study materials. Also, remove souvenirs, photographs, even text books from other classes. Clear off anything that might take your thoughts away from your current topic of study.

Exercise 1

Go to your study space. Look at everything on the work surface and everything you can see while studying. How many of these objects do you actually need for your upcoming study session? How much can you see that might distract your mind from the materials you intend to study? Remove those objects and put them out of the line of sight.

What is the one thing you should add to your study area to make it more effective? This is a trick question. The answer is "nothing." It is more likely that you will have to remove objects from your study area in order to concentrate better. Clear away anything you will not be studying during a particular session. The only objects you need for your study session are a desk or table, chair, light, and your study materials for one class. Nearby, out of your line of vision, you can store materials for other classes.

Exercise 2

Now that the top of your desk or table is clear, look around the rest of the area. Make it difficult to see anything but what you are studying at that moment. Put your desk or work table facing a blank wall. Have a storage place (book shelf, cabinet, whatever) with your books and supplies from all your classes nearby but out of sight. Being reminded of other subjects you need to study may cause you to vacillate between your planned present study topic and some other topic you plan to study at a different time.

Have a strong light directly over your study materials. If you are easily distracted, it may help to turn off other lights in the room and leave only the strong lamp over your workspace. The focus of light serves to point attention with laser-like intensity only on where it is shining.

"Way to go!"

Factor 4 — Internal Distractions

Internal distractions can be pleasant or unpleasant. Happy internal distractions might include wishing you were at the beach with a special friend or thinking about what to wear to an upcoming social event. Frequently, internal distractions are less pleasant.

Worry is enormously distracting. Nursing students often have much to worry about besides their studies: Relationships, family problems, and financial concerns. If they do not already have a partner, nursing students are in the age-range when it is natural to be thinking about long-term relationships. Nursing students' parents may be facing the emotional or health problems of aging, which could cause worrisome thoughts.

A student once said he had difficulty concentrating while studying at his desk, because his thoughts kept drifting off to financial concerns. Some exploration revealed that his financial worries were being cued by a stack of unpaid bills that he kept in a basket on the corner of his desk. Whenever his eyes wandered over to that spot, his thoughts quite naturally drifted away from his studies and toward his debts. Once he placed the bills in a desk drawer, his ability to concentrate improved dramatically!

If you are plagued with internal distractions, the following exercises can help.

Exercise 1

Keep a note card or a scrap of paper to record straying thoughts. Each time you catch your thoughts wandering away from your studies, write down the subject of your wandering thoughts. Is there a pattern? Look for cues near your study area that might be causing your thoughts to stray.

Exercise 2

Silly as it sounds, this exercise works! If your "stray thoughts" show a persistent pattern of worry, get out your schedule and set a specific time to worry (or deal with) that problem. If it is a problem that you can resolve, take care of it at the scheduled time. If it's worrying about something over which you have no control (all too often the case), schedule the time anyway. Tell yourself you'll worry about it at the scheduled time and get back to your studies. Then absolutely follow through on your plan to worry at the scheduled time.

We think you'll have a hard time worrying on schedule, but go ahead and try anyway. You will have accomplished two important things: 1) Knowing you have set aside the time to think about the problem lets you get back to your studying; 2) If you discover you can't really worry on schedule, you will have learned from experience the futility of worrying about something over which you have no control.

Exercise 3

Unwanted thoughts creep up on you unconsciously. Your mind may have been off someplace else for ten minutes when you meant to be studying. Watch out for unwanted or straying thoughts and zap them as soon as you become aware that your attention has wandered. One student wore a rubber band on her wrist and gave it a small "pop" the instant she realized her thoughts had drifted to a persistent problem. The zap from the rubber band immediately gave her a slight punishment for wasting time by not concentrating on her studies. If you use this technique, don't pop the rubber band so hard that you hurt yourself, just enough to remind you to keep focused on your work.

Exercise 4

You can argue yourself out of wasting study time. As soon as you catch yourself daydreaming or worrying or whatever you do when you stop thinking about your work, put your study materials to one side. On a piece of scratch paper or a note card, write down what you were doing (daydreaming, worrying, etc.). Then write down, or say, all the reasons why you should not be doing that (waste of time, keep from studying, useless, etc.) Give yourself counter-arguments about the disruptive thought. Remind yourself that your study time is sacred. Return to your studies only when you are certain that your thoughts are under control and you are ready to concentrate on your work.

Factor 5 — Working at a Fast Pace

It may sound counter-intuitive, but keeping up a quick pace as you study helps your concentration. You may be thinking, "No way! How can I really think about what I'm studying if I'm in a race with time?" True, there will be occasions when you really have to think about the material you're studying, for example, to understand a complicated under-lying physiological process. Obviously, you should slow down at that point.

Why does keeping up a quick pace help concentra-tion? Because working quickly focuses attention on the task at hand and does not permit straying thoughts. If you have learned how to speed read, you will know that you cannot think of anything but what you're reading when you read with a sense of urgency. Urgency makes the job more excit-ing. It's almost impossible to feel bored when you are work-ing as fast as you can.

Exercise 1

Use a timer for this exercise. As you begin your study session, decide how quickly you want to accomplish each task. Here's an example: in a two-hour evening session, you may decide first to pre-read fifteen minutes for tomorrow morning's lec-ture in Pathophysiology and then spend one hour and 45 min-utes reading and making notes for today's lecture in Adult Health Care. After you have completed the prereading, time yourself as you read one page of your Adult Health Care text and multiply the number of pages to be read by that amount of time to decide how many pages you can finish in the allot-ted time. As an example, if you can read one page in five min-utes, you can get through twelve pages in one hour. Then you have 45 minutes to make notes on those twelve pages. It's amaz-ing how much a deadline focuses attention on your work

Exercise 2

As you read, use a straight edge (like a ruler or a note-card) to cover the text you have just read and keep moving it down the page at a steady rate. This technique will help force your eyes down the page. By covering up what you just read, you will be less tempted to re-read. Check the timer periodically to be sure you are completing the tasks on time. You defi-nitely won't be daydreaming or dozing.

Factor 6 — Ability to Study
for Extended Periods

When you were in high school, you may have thought an hour was a very long time for a study session. College students are usually able to sit and study for a couple hours at a time. Nursing students must be able to focus their attention for at least two hours and often much longer. Endurance for concentrating on study materials is a learned ability and improves with practice. It also helps to vary your study method during a long session of concentrated study. For example, during an extended evening study session, you could begin with fifteen minutes of pre-reading for tomorrow. Then you could read and make notes over material presented in today's lectures.

Finally, you could do a review over some notes you made yesterday. Or, to raise your motivation, you could insert a short self-test in the middle of a long reading and note-making session.

An interesting biological aspect of scheduling two-hour study sessions comes from the research on ultradian rhythms. These are natural hormonal fluctuations that occur every 90-120 minutes day and night in both men and women. Between each of these 90-120 minute periods of maximum wakefulness and concentration, there are 20 minute "troughs" where it is difficult to assimilate new information. That's the ideal time for a study break!

Exercise 1

Challenge yourself to increase your endurance for longer periods of study. Try to extend your regular time by a half hour. Then after a week or so, add in another half hour. Soon you should be able to study for three to four hours with only one or two short breaks.

Exercise 2

Reward yourself at the end of a long study session. Look over how much you have accomplished and tell yourself how pleased you are to have done so much. Congratulate yourself on how much you have learned. Take a break and know that you deserve it.

Factor 7—Cues to Start Studying: "Time to Study" Rituals

An environmental cue is also called a discriminative stimulus. These cues can be places, times, or objects. This is why we say that you should not study while lying down on a bed or sofa. Beds and sofas are stimuli for rest and relaxation, exactly what you do *not* want to do when you are studying. We recommend strongly that you have a special place to study at home and also a particular place where you always study at school, for example, a library carrel. The place, if you always study there, is in itself a cue for studying.

Activities can also provide cues to what will follow. Most people have a "getting ready for bed" routine, such as, brushing your teeth, washing your face, putting on your p.j.'s, setting an alarm clock, etc. "Time to study" rituals could include: clearing your study area, getting out your study materials, positioning your desk lamp, turning off your cell phone, etc.

Time can also cue an activity. If you look at a clock and see that it's noon, you're likely to think, "I need to get some lunch." As far as possible, use the power of discriminative stimuli of specific times and places to get you quickly into your studies. For example, if you regularly study between 7:30 p.m. and 10 p.m. at your special study desk or table, you will find that you can immediately settle into your study session when you sit down there at 7:30 p.m. The place and the time combine to form a powerful cue to get involved in your work quickly.

CHAPTER 6

Exercise 1

If you don't already have one, set up a special place to study at home, a place where, preferably, you do nothing else but study. The simpler the set-up, the better. You need nothing but a desk or table, a chair and a lamp, preferably with the desk or table facing the wall. If your home is too small for a special study room, consider converting a large (walk-in type) closet into a study space. Or clear out a section of a storage room and box it in with bookcases. Don't put anything in your study space that doesn't cue studying.

Exercise 2

Find a spot at school where you can regularly study. The library is an obvious choice, but you may also find a quiet place in a cafeteria or a classroom that is not being used at the specific times you want to study - perhaps when you have an hour or two between lectures. Look around the school at those times to see what place would be available and quiet. Then study at that place regularly.

"Looks like this student needs to work on Factors 1 and 7."

 **Evaluation**

Exercise — Monitor Your Concentration for One Week

In each of the boxes in the following chart, estimate your level of concentration (as percentage of time fully focusing on your work).

	Morning Session	Afternoon Session	Evening Session	Your Daily Average
Monday	%	%	%	%
Tuesday	%	%	%	%
Wednesday	%	%	%	%
Thursday	%	%	%	%
Friday	%	%	%	%
Saturday	%	%	%	%
Sunday	%	%	%	%

Check-up for the Concentration Exercise

After monitoring your concentration for one week, answer the following questions.

1. Do you see a pattern in your levels of concentration? When is your concentration best? When is it lowest?

_____

_____

_____

2. Can you identify the reason *why* your concentration was lower during certain study sessions? Which of the seven concentration factors could have been related to this drop in concentration?

3. What do you need to do to improve your ability to focus at those times or places?

Study Area Checklist

Your study area should include the following elements:

- Desk or table
- Lamp or good overhead lighting
- Chair that promotes good posture
- Only the materials for the one subject you are studying
- Comfortable temperature

Your study area should *not* include:

- Pictures of loved ones
- Other study materials (nothing on the desk except what you are studying at that moment)
- Bills or other financial statements
- An inviting view of the out-of-doors
- Anything that cues you to think of something besides the topic you are studying.

 # Summary

Students get used to many distractions in their study environment and are often surprised to find how much time they can save when they eliminate these problems and raise their level of concentration. You could possibly sit next to a busy freeway or in a cage full of seagulls and study, but how efficient would that be? Focusing on the work at hand will save time for all the rest of your busy life. Learn which of the seven concentration factors most affects your own ability to focus and use that information to help increase your ability to concentrate.

↑ Concentration = ↑ Comprehension & ↓ Study Time!

 # Student Feedback

Below are a variety of students' responses to the concentration evaluation. Can you identify the concentration factor involved in each comment?

I concentrate better when I tell myself that I want to study and want to do well.

I need to cut off the TV when I study.

I concentrate better when I don't worry about what class to study for.

I do better when I go someplace quiet and where I have no choice but to study.

I concentrate better and am more focused in the middle of a study period, when I have all my information organized.

I find that I concentrate better in the evenings and when I'm feeling less stressed.

I need to remember to eat well and keep hydrated so I don't get headaches.

I need to encourage myself about whatever it is I am studying, instead of being distracted by negative thoughts.

I concentrate better in the morning when my mind is fresh.

If I can begin my study period with some meditation, my concentration is much better.

I am learning to put off other thoughts and worries until after my study time is over for the day.

When I schedule time to take care of my obligations, then I can study and concentrate without interruptions.

When I discipline myself to keep my study time as my study time and nothing else, I can pay close attention and stay focused.

 ## References

Baker, R.W., & Madell, T. (1965). Susceptibility to distraction in academically underachieving male college students. *Journal of Consulting Psychology*, 29, 173-177.

> Underachieving college students are more susceptible to distraction when studying, e.g., conversations or background noise.

Challem, J. (2006). *The Nutrition Reporter*. Retrieved from www.nutritionreporter.com

> Monthly review of clinical research on vitamin, mineral and food therapies.

Collins, K.W., Dansereau, D.F., Holley, C.D., & Brooks, L.W. (1981). Control of concentration during academic tasks. *Journal of Educational Psychology, 73,* 122-128.
Productive self-talk was found to enhance comprehension and retention of textual material.

Dux, P.E., Invanoff, J., Asplund, C.L. & Marois, R. (2006). Isolation of a central bottleneck of information processing with time-resolved fMRI. *Neuron, 52,* 1109-1120.

Research on the effects of multi-taking. There appears to be a central bottleneck in the brain that prevents us from being able to do two things at once.

Egoscue, P. (1988). *Pain free: A revolutionary method for stopping chronic pain.* New York: Bantam Books.

Stretches to help relieve and prevent chronic pain. Written by a physical therapist. Also authored *Pain free at your PC.*

Gibbs, J.J. (1990). *Dancing with your books: The zen way of studying.* New York: Penguin Books.

Presents Zen methods of increasing concentration while you study.

Mednick, S.C., & Ehrman, M. (2006). *Take a nap! Change your life.* New York: Workman Publishing.

This book discusses the research on the benefits of napping and shows you how to plan the optimum nap to increase alertness, strengthen memory and reduce stress.

Oetting, E. (1964). Hypnosis and concentration in study. *American Journal of Clinical Hypnosis, 7,* 148-151.

Research study shows hypnosis can improve study concentration. This article gives examples of hypnotic suggestions that students could use.

Robinson, F.P. (1970). *Effective study.* New York: Harper and Row.

Chapter on importance of concentration with some suggestions to improve it.

Rossi, E.L. (1991). *The 20 minute break: Reduce stress, maximize performance, and improve health and emotional well-being using the new science of ultradian rhythms.* Los Angeles: Jeremy P. Tarcher, Inc.

How our daily ultradian rhythms affect levels of concentration and well-being.

Talley, J.E., & Henning, L.H. (1981). *Study skills*. Springfield, MA: Charles C. Thomas.
Chapter on importance of concentration with specific suggestions to improve it.

Vital Skills

Productive Self-Talk and Anxiety Management

(Week 5)

> I put up a sign on the wall in front of where I study. On it is written, 'I can do this!'

 Assessment: Self-Talk

*Directions: Following are thoughts some students report while **preparing for** or **during** a test. Indicate how often you have similar thoughts by circling the appropriate number to the left of each statement.*

Always
Often
Sometimes
Rarely
Never

4 ③ 2 1 0   1. "I must get an 'A' on this test."

4 3 2 1 ⓪   2. "I am worthless if I don't get a good grade on this test."

4 3 ② 1 0   3. "I am dumb."

4 3 ② 1 0   4. "There is too much information in my notes. It's too much. I can't remember it all."

4 3 2 ① 0   5. "I'm not going to pass."

4 3 2 1 ⓪   6. "I have no future if I fail this test."

CHAPTER 7

Always	Often	Sometimes	Rarely	Never	
4	3	2	1	**(0)**	7. "I must aim for a perfect test score."
4	3	2	**(1)**	0	8. "Why can't this be easier? Why does my life have to be so hard?"
4	**(3)**	2	1	0	9. As I go through the test, I keep thinking about the items I have already missed.
4	3	2	1	**(0)**	10. I look at the other students taking the test and think they are probably doing better than me.
4	3	2	**(1)**	0	11. My first reaction to reading a difficult item is "I can *not* do this!"
4	**(3)**	2	1	0	12. My mind wanders and I find myself wishing I were doing something other than the test in front of me. For example, I might look out the window and wish I were enjoying myself outdoors.
4	3	2	1	**(0)**	13. I worry about what others will think of me when they find out how I did on the test.
4	3	**(2)**	1	0	14. I keep thinking, "I am not going to pass."
(4)	**(3)**	2	1	0	15. I want to run out of the room and never come back. I think, "Let me out of here!"

_____

Total Score *(Add the numbers you circled.)*

Score Interpretation — Self-Talk

You earn congratulations if your score was less than 15

points. You are not your own worst enemy while preparing for, or during, a test. Good for you!

If your total was more than 25, go over this chapter repeatedly.

If your score was over 35, personal counseling at your school counseling center is also recommended. You will be a happier, more productive person when you stop making yourself miserable with negative thoughts.

Goal: Learn To Be Your Own Best Friend

Your goals in working through this chapter are to understand how unconscious thoughts can cause problems, learn to bring a negative thought into awareness, replace it with a more useful thought, and to set up a feedback system that will let you know you are on track.

Rationale

Anxiety is an all-encompassing feeling of fear, which can have emotional, cognitive, and physical symptoms. The greater the sense of threat, the more serious the symptoms.

For most students, the levels of anxiety are in the mild to moderate range, but they can still cause functional problems in all three areas. Emotionally, people can become more irritable, angry, sad, withdrawn, or apathetic. Cognitively, they may lose concentration, be more easily distracted, remember less, or use poor judgment in decision-making. Physically, they experience different levels of the "fight or flight" syndrome, including rapid heart rate, perspiration, faster breathing, and muscular tension. Biologically, our bodies have evolved to deal with threat by physical effort—either running away or fighting the enemy. It is not possible, however, for people to deal with most contemporary threats, such as taking a test or driving in heavy traffic, by either fleeing or fighting. So, how can we deal with our modern stressors?

Decisions about what is threatening occur in the frontal cortex of the brain. Your brain decides what poses a threat and the anxious responses follow. It all begins with your perception of threat. The physical responses follow that thought.

Don't We Need Motivation When Faced With Difficult Tasks?

Yes, but let's not confuse motivation (moderate increase in the fight or flight response) with serious anxiety or fear. The relationship between motivation and fear to performance is well-documented and has been known for almost a century.

If there is little or no motivation, performance is low. As motivation increases, so does performance—up to a point. When motivation becomes too high we call it "anxiety" and performance begins to decrease. At the extreme of fear, a person can become incapable of any productive action. Have you ever heard of the term "scared stiff"?

Motivation Curve

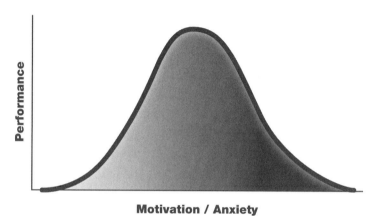

Motivation / Anxiety

Figure 7.1

Test Anxiety

Some students may see tests as a threat. After all, you must at least pass it, or there will be unpleasant consequences. It is sometimes hard to know whether that perception is realistic (the student knows he has not studied properly) or unrealistic, based on erroneous or dysfunctional thinking, for example, "I must be perfect." The results are the same in either case. The over-anxious student is highly distractible, is nervous and has difficulty focusing on review materials prior to the test and on test questions during the test. The student whose motivation is within reasonable bounds is able to concentrate on the task at hand.

Most people are more aware of their physical symptoms of anxiety than they are of the thoughts that cause them. It is, however, much more efficient to attack the root causes of anxiety (thoughts) than to work on the obvious manifestations of anxiety (physical symptoms). The trick is to identify negative thoughts early, before they have a chance to put your body on red alert, and to replace them with more positive or, at least, more useful, thoughts.

You *Can* Change the Way You Think

Good news! Controlling negative thinking is just like getting control of any other behavior. Negative thinking patterns are often just bad habits. True, you have probably learned them over a lifetime, so they are rather deeply imbedded habits. Some of them may have come from your family. Parents sometimes pass negative thoughts on to their children (For example, "Don't try to do that. It's too hard for you"), and, in that sense, they are "inherited," but they are definitely not in your genes.

They are learned behaviors. Since you learned them, you can also unlearn them and replace unproductive thoughts with more productive thoughts in almost any situation. You <u>can</u> change a "bad attitude" and possibly even look forward to academic challenges.

Regarding "attitude," students often find that the rigors of a nursing program cause them to reexamine the spiritual dimension of their lives. Many choose to incorporate their spiritual practices, such as prayer or meditation into their study habits. You may also find it helpful to emulate a positive role-model, perhaps a mentor, or even a fellow student. Draw from all the resources that encourage you to do your best!

The following chart outlines the seven main types of negative, unproductive thoughts and their consequences.

Seven Types of Negative, Unproductive Thoughts and Possible Consequences

	Negative, Unproductive Thoughts	Possible Emotional or Behavorial Consequences
1	If I am *not perfect*, I am a total loser. There is nothing in between being on the top rung of perfection and the absolute bottom of the ladder in life. I must always fight for the top position.	Anxiety, lack of focus, making careless errors due to worrying.
2	I am *helpless* to do anything about my situation. My life is totally controlled by outside forces. I cannot, therefore, solve any problem. I can do nothing to help myself. I am no good at (fill in the blank).	Depression, give up, don't keep working on the task.
3	I'm *not good enough*. I will never succeed. Any failure only confirms my fundamental belief in my own worthlessness. I can't understand how I got into nursing school. They must have mixed up the applications in the admissions office. I don't belong here.	Depression, give up, feel tired.
4	Other *people are bad*. Other people cause all my problems. Any problem I have is all the fault of someone else. They are out to get me!	Anger, complaining, friends avoid spending time with you.
5	*I can't stand it*. It is awful. It is unbearable. It'll kill me (whatever it is).	Fear, avoid the task. One student actually ran out of the room at the beginning of a test.
6	*If only*... I were a prince or princess and had a fairy godmother. Things should be better or easier for me. Why should life be so hard for me? Things should come to me without effort on my part. Why can't I just be 'discovered' and become rich and famous without all this hassle? I deserve a better life. I'd be happier basking on a sunny beach, hiking up a beautiful mountain, eating in a four star restaurant. I shouldn't have to work so hard.	Lethargy, daydreaming, wasting time, loss of concentration.
7	*I am doomed*. A bad fairy presided over my birth, and now my life is cursed. I'll never be lucky. Sooner or later, some terrible thing is going to happen to me. This type wears his/her personal rain cloud. Nothing will ever go right. I'm doomed to fail! There is nothing I can do to change my horrible fate. Of course, I'll never achieve my goal of becoming a nurse.	Depression, dread, chronic worrying, distraction.

If any of these types of negative thoughts are hanging around in your head, you will not be working at your best while studying or taking a test. Imagine trying to concentrate on reviewing your notes while part of your brain is saying, "Why try? You're a loser."

"I can't stand it" keeps you from persisting in the task. It's easier to give up if you feel a little frustrated or tired and go watch an old movie on television or call a friend. It's also sometimes a reason students leave tests early, before they have a chance to review their answers and make sure they have not made any careless errors. They think, "I can't stand this one more minute. Get me out of here."

If you think the task is a monster ("It's driving me crazy!"), you could be justified in doing anything else, even least favorite tasks like dish-washing and vacuum-cleaning, to avoid it.

Perhaps inevitable doom is the worst of them. The student goes from "I don't know if I'll remember this factoid on the test," to "Then I'll flunk the test," to "Then I'll fail the course," to "Then I'll be expelled from nursing school," to "Then my life will be ruined." These thoughts can occur with the speed of an avalanche. You aren't even aware of how you got from the beginning "Will I remember?" to "My life is ruined."

A champion negative thinker can use all seven types of negative thoughts, but most of us stick with one or two favorite kinds. That favorite negative thought, over time and with many repetitions, can eventually become part of the "personality". And all this is below the level of consciousness.

Are you ready to make a change? The steps in stopping negative, unproductive thinking are:

A. Identify the situation or activating event (e.g., taking a test) in which the negative thought occurs.

B. Identify the underlying thought ("I'm going to fail"). This is sometimes hard at first but gets easier with practice.

C. Notice the consequence of your negative thought (stop concentrating, start perspiring, etc.).

 Interventions

Exercise 1 — Learning to Identify Negative, Unproductive Thoughts

In each of the following scenarios, the situation or *activating event* (A) is identified for you, as is the emotional, physical, or behavioral *consequence* (C) of the negative thought. Your task is to write in the blank what negative thought or *belief* (B) might logically fit in that sequence.

A. Activating Event: Sal is sitting in lecture, and the student sitting in the next seat turns with a smile and asks, "Are you ready for the test tomorrow?"

B. Belief/Thought: Sal thinks _____

C. Consequence: Sal squirms, tenses, swallows hard, looks away and takes a long time to respond.

A. Activating Event: Carol sits at desk at home, preparing for a major test.

B. Belief/Thought: Carol thinks_____

C. Consequence: Carol begins to cry.

A. Activating Event: During a final examination, Chris keeps looking around the room at other students industriously answering test questions.

B. Belief/Thought: Chris thinks_____

C. Consequence: Chris goes blank and starts to perspire.

———•—•———

Many of us, when asked if we have negative or unproductive thoughts, would answer, "Not me! I'm an upbeat sort of person." Still, most of us occasionally feel down, angry, hurt, or any of a host of unpleasant emotions. Negative thoughts always precede the unpleasant emotions.

Exercise 2 — Identifying Your Own Patterns of Negative, Unproductive Thinking

To identify your own patterns of thinking, carry a small notebook for one week. Every time you experience any unpleasant emotion, write down the situation, what you thought, and your emotional reaction. You will probably find that the same type of negative self-talk repeats and repeats in your brain.

After one week, return to this page and answer the questions below.

 **Evaluation**

Check-up for Exercise 2 — Identifying Your Own Patterns

What did you learn this week about the relationship between your thoughts and your feelings? Any patterns?

_____

_____

_____

_____

Convincing Yourself to Discard Your Negative, Unproductive Thoughts

If you have developed a long-term habit of a certain type of negative or unproductive thinking, it may take some work for you to give it up. You have just spent a week analyzing how your own emotions may be related to your thoughts. If you have identified a persistent thought that causes you trouble, you can put that thought to the test *now*.

First, ask yourself, **is it true**? Let's imagine, for example, that you have an unproductive thought of the "I'm doomed to fail" variety. If you are in nursing school, clearly some people thought you had a good chance to succeed, or you would not have been admitted. It may be true that the nursing school curriculum is more difficult than courses you took previously, and you have to work harder now in order to succeed, but is it really true that you are doomed to fail? Most, of the other students in your class are probably working harder now than they did in their previous course work. Are they all doomed to fail? So a true replacement statement might be, "This may be harder than my other classes, but I will just have to work harder." That statement would have quite different emotional and behavioral consequences, wouldn't it?

Second, ask yourself, even if there is some grain of truth in the statement (that is, it is possible that I could fail), **is it useful** to say it to myself while I am studying or taking an exam? The answer to that question is surely a resounding, "No!" If you were at the starting block of a race with a dozen

CHAPTER 7

other racers around you, it would be true that you might not win. After all, only one person can win a race, and it might be one of the others in the race with you. But how useful is it to think, "I could lose this race," at the starting line?

Lastly, does thinking negatively help you **achieve your goals** in life? No. No matter what your goals, negative thinking can only put stumbling blocks in your way. If your unproductive thoughts lead to unhappiness and physical symptoms of stress, they are certainly not helping you along the path you've chosen for your life.

We hope that asking yourself these three questions about your negative thoughts will convince you to change the thought to one that is true, useful and gets you where you want to go in life.

Replacing Unproductive or Negative Thoughts

If unproductive thinking is occasionally making you feel depressed, anxious or worried, you can learn to change to more productive thinking. You can become happier, calmer, more energetic, more motivated, and more confident by replacing negative thoughts with positive thoughts that are also realistic.

The replacement thoughts cannot be unbelievable, or you'll quickly discard them and go right back to the original negative thought. If you were thinking, "I'm going to fail the test," and feeling anxious or discouraged, you can't simply say, "I'm going to get a perfect score." You will not believe the new thought. But you *could* say, "I'm going to do my best. I'm going to give it my best shot." That is an entirely realistic idea and will lead to feeling more motivated—a feeling that is useful when you have to put out a lot of effort reviewing for a test.

Finding good replacement thoughts may not be easy at first. We offer some ideas to help you come up with good ones.

Three Tips for Choosing Replacement Thoughts

1. Use only *positive* words in the replacement thought. For example, if you are thinking, "I am going to fail this test," you would not replace it with, "I won't fail this test." The words "fail" and "won't" are both negative. Better would be something about how much effort you are putting into studying or how much your studying is improving now that you are making such excellent study notes: "I am working hard at my studies" or "I'm improving my study habits."

2. If you can't come up with something positive in the situation, try for something that at least is *neutral.* For example, "I am getting better."

3. Make sure you *believe* your replacement thought. For example, try something along the lines of "Most of the class will pass the test, so I probably will, too." It's enough to point yourself in the direction you want to go.

Replacing Your Negative, Unproductive Thoughts Is As Easy As A, B, C, D

One student kept telling himself that the information he was studying for a particular course would never be of any use to him later when he would be working as a nurse. Saying that to himself naturally made him feel annoyed ("What a waste of time!") and could easily lead to avoid studying that subject. After he identified his negative thought, he replaced it by telling himself, "Maybe there's a good reason they want us to learn this. I'll probably find out later where this information fits in when I take other courses. Then I'll be glad I learned it."

If you identified any unproductive thoughts in the Intervention earlier in the chapter, the next exercise will help you, especially if you saw a repetitive pattern of the same type of negative thoughts.

Do the exercise below in the five to seven days preceding a test. The stress of preparing for a test is likely to make your favorite negative thought occur. You will be doing this exercise repeatedly, because, remember, negative thinking patterns are deeply embedded habits, and repetition will be required to remove them. The repetition may seem a little boring, but boring is good. Boring is at least not anxiety, quite the opposite. Over that week, you should have talked yourself out of your useless negative thought. Here's what to do every time the unproductive thought appears:

Exercise — Replacing Unproductive Thoughts By Arguing With Yourself

Directions: Use the "Replacing Negative, Unproductive Thoughts" worksheet on page 180 to complete this exercise.

First, identify the situation, which will be labeled "A" for activating event. Then say aloud the bothersome thought "B", which stands for underlying belief. This keeps the thought from lurking unnoticed and brings it out into the open. For example, you might say out loud: "There's no way I'm going to pass the pathophysiology test next week." In saying it aloud, or writing it down, you are, as it were, facing down the enemy.

Next, think about how you feel or act whenever you have that thought. Does it make you tense, depressed, avoid looking at your pathophysiology text or notes? "C" stands for "consider the consequences." Write the consequences of your belief under C.

Third, go through the three "convince yourself" questions. "D" is for debate and decision.

- Is it *true* that you can't possibly pass your pathophysiology exam? Or is your self-talk an exaggeration?

- Is it *useful* to keep telling yourself this unproductive message? Not likely. It makes you feel bad in any number of ways.

- Will it help you pass the test (*achieve your goal*) to keep saying that to yourself? Certainly not.

So, you decide to replace the "I can't pass" thought with something more useful and also believable. Write your decision after "D" on the worksheet.

Finally, write your replacement thought in the last blank and repeat it to yourself every time the negative thought recurs.

Worksheet — Replacing Negative, Unproductive Thoughts

A. Activating event (the situation in which the thought occurs):

_____

_____

B. Belief or bothersome thought in that situation:

_____

_____

C. Consequence (can be emotional or behavioral or both):

_____

_____

D. Dispute and decide (is the belief *true, useful, help* me get where I want to go?):

_____

_____

E. Replacement thought/belief:

_____

_____

Short Cut

Once you have done the hard work and learned to be aware of negative or unproductive thinking, you may be able to take a "short-cut" to getting rid of that thought. Some people find that physical movement can help them discard a thought and reorient their thinking.

Have you ever seen a person quickly shake her head when she's heard or thought something unpleasant? That's a gesture you can use as a "short cut". A simple physical change like sitting down or standing up, a shake of the head or putting your hands to your face can be your signal to change "channels" in your thinking. Even moving your eyes—literally "shifting your focus" to a different object—can help change the way you look at things.

Check-Up for Replacing Negative, Unproductive Thoughts Worksheet

Briefly describe what you have learned about identifying and replacing unproductive thoughts. Is this something that is easy or difficult for you to do?

_____

_____

_____

_____

_____

_____

_____

_____

_____

CHAPTER 7

Part II: Self-Talk and Anxiety Management

 ## Assessment: Physical Symptoms of Anxiety

Physical symptoms can help you identify negative, unproductive thinking.

Put a check mark in front of any or all of the physical symptoms that sometimes or often apply to you just prior to or during and exam.

_____ Skin flushing or rash
_____ Hand trembling or unsteadiness of legs
_____ Nausea
_____ Chest pain
_____ Ragged breathing
_____ Dizziness
_____ Difficulty swallowing or dry mouth
_____ Chills
_____ Rapid heart rate
_____ Excessive perspiration
_____ Headache
_____ Neck or back pain

If any of the above symptoms of physical tension occur regularly immediately preceding and during exams, go to your school counseling center. The staff can probably provide some form of **relaxation training**, either individually, in a group, or by audio recording. Feeling anxious, especially in testing situation, is so common for students that school counseling centers typically offer a variety of programs to deal with it.

Decades of research attest to the success of these programs. They are offered as a service to you, usually without any charge, so you might as well take advantage of them. There are also a myriad of books and audio recordings you can buy or check out from libraries and refer to whenever tension causes physical discomfort.

Meanwhile, use the physical symptoms as clues to when you are having a problematic thought. You may be unaware of the underlying thought, but it's hard to ignore trembling hands or the sudden onset of nausea.

Mastery = Getting from Negativity to Actual Enjoyment

Once there was a woman who hated folding and putting away laundry. The trouble was that she had a husband and two small children who could create many loads of laundry every week. As long as she told herself that she hated to fold it and put it away when it came out of the dryer, clothes piled up everywhere, on sofas, beds, in baskets.

One day she dropped in on a friend who was in the midst of folding laundry. The friend said, "I just love folding clean clothes and putting them in drawers. Clean clothes smell so good. They look so neat when they're folded nicely. And it's wonderful to open a drawer filled with neatly folded, clean clothes. It's my favorite household job." This was an eye-opener! The woman went home and said all those same statements to herself as she put the finishing touches on her laundry.

People can now sit on the sofa at her house. The family doesn't have to remove piles of clean clothes from the bed before they go to sleep at night. They can easily find their clothing in their closets and drawers. What had she done to accomplish this miracle? She started saying, "I love to fold clothes and put them away!" The more she said it, the more she believed it. She had gone far beyond getting rid of a negative thought. She became a positive thinker, at least about doing laundry.

The moral of this story can apply to anything that you must do but put off because you tell yourself you don't like it. If you can learn to love doing laundry, you can learn to love many things. Perhaps you don't get enough exercise, because you think exercise routines are boring. You can go on beyond neutral, which could be something like "I'll feel healthier after I exercise today." You can get to positively enjoying your workout. You can think, "No day is complete until I've had my exercise" or "I'm addicted to my daily walk."

You can get past neutral to positive with studying and test-taking, too. You can actually look forward to a pleasant evening of reading your assignments. You can take delight in creating a beautiful set of notes. Beautiful notes are a joy to behold. When you feel happy for the opportunity to show what you have learned as you take a test, you will be a world-class positive thinker. You wanted to become a nursing student. Now enjoy it!

 Intervention: Part II

Exercise 3 — Make Encouragement Cards

Make your own "Encouragement Cards" and post them in your study area or any other place where you will read them often.

Some ideas for cards offered by other nursing students:

I can do this!
I have a great study system and know what to do next.
What one person can do, another can, too!
This information is important.

This information will be useful to me in other classes and on the NCLEX.

Make hay while the sun shines!

This is my study time. I will focus on studying now and have free time later.

Preread → Read → Make Notes → Review → Self Test → Succeed!

Learning this will help me be a better nurse.

Knowing this information could save someone's life.

"Encourage yourself."

Evaluation: Part II

Check-Up on making Encouragement Cards.

1. What did you learn from posting some Encouragement Cards in your study area?

   _____

   _____

2. Were you able to reduce or eliminate some of your negative thoughts?

   _____

   _____

 # Summary

Much anxiety is the result of unconscious thinking. If you bring those disabling thoughts into the light of consciousness, you can then examine and replace them with more productive thoughts. Productive thoughts can help relieve anxiety and eliminate physical symptoms of stress.

 # Student Feedback

I am getting better at catching myself when I think negative thoughts. Now I can replace them with more useful thoughts.

I stay away from discouraging thoughts. I say to myself, 'You can do it,' 'Keep your head up,' 'It's getting better.'

CHAPTER 7

I used to keep telling myself how much I didn't want to read yet another chapter. Now I say to myself, 'There is a good reason I need to know this.'

I know that I will sometimes have down times, but I will succeed. I keep saying 'You can do this.'

I used to worry about getting through all the material to study. Now I say to myself, 'I have a good study system. My study system is working for me.' Now I spend more time studying and even enjoy it more.

I used to think, 'I am a real dummy.' Now I keep saying to myself, 'I'll work hard and do my best to improve my grade.' Not calling myself names improves my confidence.

I used to wish I were somewhere else when I had to study. Now I tell myself, 'This information is really interesting. I'm sure it will help me be a better nurse.' Saying that helps my concentration.

I use a grid to keep track of how many hours I am studying for each class. That way I have data. I can say, 'Look! I've studied eight hours for Patho this week.'

 # References

Balzer-Riley, J. (2004). *Communication in nursing.* (5th ed.) St. Louis, MO: Mosby.

> Chapter 22 discusses self talk and cites the work of some of the pioneers of the self-talk approach to cognitive-behavioral therapy. Not surprisingly, psychologists have discovered that self talk has a strong influence on a person's behavior.

Baumeister, R.F., Heatherton, T.F., & Tice, D.M. (1994). *Losing control: How and why people fail at self-regulation.* San Diego, CA: Academic Press.

> The authors have synthesized the research on self-regulation failure. They briefly discuss the relationship between self-esteem and self-regulation and hypothesize that lack of self-regulation may lead to lack of self-esteem. They conclude that capacity for self-regulation can be increased with effective practice.

Ellis, A. (1971). *Growth through reason*. Palo Alto, CA: Science and Behavior Books.

Ellis is the original guru of thought-stopping as a way to feel happier. His several books are written in a readable, humorous style. His work does not refer specifically to test anxiety but to living well by keeping negative thoughts under control.

Finger, R., & Gelassi, J.P. (1977). Effects of modifying cognitive vs. emotionality responses in the treatment of test anxiety. *Journal of Consulting and Clinical Psychology*, 45, 280-287.

Thought control is more effective than relaxation training in reducing test anxiety.

Goldfried, M.R., Linehand, M.M., & Smith, J.L. (1978). Reduction of test anxiety through cognitive restructuring. *Journal of Consulting and Clinical Psychology*, 46, 32-39.

College students who learned to restructure negative thoughts significantly reduced test anxiety.

Greenberg, D. (1976). *How to make yourself miserable*. New York: Random House.

A tongue-in-cheek attack on worrying. Illustrated with cartoons. The essential message is: If you are a really 'good' negative thinker, you can ruin anything.

Helmstetter, S. (1982). *What to say when you talk to your self*. New York: Pocket Books.

Discusses the five levels of Self Talk and gives specific word-for-word recommendations for constructing productive self talk. Also discusses the effectiveness of internal motivation as opposed to external motivation.

Hembrie, R. (1988). Correlates, causes, effects, and treatment of test anxiety. *Review of Educational Research*, 58, 47-77.

A thorough review of 562 studies of test anxiety. Author concludes that test anxiety can reduce test scores and also that test anxiety is correlated with negative self-evaluations and lower self-esteem.

Howard, P.J. (2000). *The owner's manual for the brain: Everyday applications from mind-brain research*. (2nd ed.) Atlanta: Bard Press.

Chapter 20 is about motivation, stress and burnout. It reviews research of each, and encourages the reader to "take charge of your life." Includes Martin Seligman's research from his book *Learned Optimism*.

Maultsby, M. (1975). *Help yourself to happiness*. New York: Institute of Rational Emotive Therapy.

A good introduction to thought control for the general reader. Maultsby was a student of Ellis' earlier work.

Yerkes, R.M. & Dodson, J.D. (1908). The relation of strength of stimulus to rapidity of habit formation. *Journal of Comparative Neurology*, 18, 458-482.

Review of studies of the earlier "motivation curve." While low motivation leads to low performance, very high motivation, experienced as nervousness or tension, can have the same result. Moderate motivation leads to best performance.

CHAPTER 7

Smart Test-Taking Strategies

(Week 6)

> *Tests aren't so bad when you really know the material.*

Assessment: How Do You Take Tests Now?

Never
Rarely
Sometimes
Often
Always

Directions: Mark the number that describes your current system of test-taking.

④ 3 2 1 0   1. I am easily distracted by other students in the room while taking a test.

④ 3 2 1 0   2. On a paper-and-pencil test, I begin with the first question and answer each ques tion in order straight through the test.

④ 3 2 1 0   3. I leave the testing room as soon as I am finished answering the last question, even if there is more tie ver me allowed.

0 1 2 3 ④   4. If I'm not sure of the answer, I guess, but only if there is no penalty for guessing.

0 1 2 3 ④   5. On multiple choice questions, I look at each answer as a separate true or false option.

CHAPTER 8

4 3 2 ①0   6. I keep worrying about how many questions I may have answered incorrectly as I take a test.

0 1 ②3 4   7. In reviewing my responses to the test questions, I change the answers on the chance that my first answer was wrong.

4 3 ②1 0   8. While answering a multiple choice option, I think of exceptions to the rule or special cases.

④3 2 1 0   9. Due to late night cramming, I get very little sleep just before a test.

4 ③2 1 ⓪   10. I spend time immediately before an exam quizzing my classmates, or having them quiz me over the material.

0 1 2 3 ④   11. When taking a paper-and-pencil test, I circle or underline key words in the question, before looking at the possible answers.

0 ①2 3 4   12. When I know how many questions will be on the exam, I calculate how much time to spend on each question.

0 1 2 3 ④   13. I pay special attention when a test item is negatively worded (e.g., not, except, all but, etc.).

0 1 2 ③4   14. When I am not sure of the correct answer, I write or bring to mind the key facts that I know about the topic, and

then look for relationships between
what I do know and the options given.

0 1 2 3 4   15. When I have to guess at an answer, I
look in the question and options for
clues to what is correct.

0 1 2 3 4   16. If there is no penalty for guessing, and
there is only one minute remaining of test
time with 10 questions unanswered, I do
not leave them blank. I just "bubble in" a
response without even reading the
question.

0 1 2 3 4   17. When I have the opportunity to look
over a corrected test, I review the incorrect answers to see why I missed them.

4 3 2 1 0   18. I consume too much caffeine and do not
take time to eat regular meals before
major exams.

4 3 2 1 0   19. I get bogged down on a difficult question and spend too much time trying to
figure out the answer.

4 3 2 1 0   20. I run out of time on classroom tests.

Total Score (*Add the numbers circled above.*)

Feedback on Test-Taking Answers

Assess your test-taking skill by comparing your answers to
the responses on the following page.

CHAPTER 8

1. Remember everything you learned about keeping focused? You need to attend to your own test. If this is difficult, consider wearing earplugs or choosing a seat where you are least likely to be disturbed by others in the room. For example, in a lecture class, if you sit on the front row, you will not see so many other students.

2. Your mantra should be: "Answer the Easy Ones First!"(AEOF) This will help you build your self-confidence as you take the exam and will allow time for questions that are more difficult. It you are taking a computerized exam which does not allow moving back and forth between items, then of course you don't have that option. But do not linger too long (no more than 2 minutes) on any one item, or you risk not completing the exam.

3. If you finish early, use the extra time on a paper-and-pencil exam to review your answers. Make sure your all your marks correspond to the numbers of the questions. Get in the habit of checking every tenth question. You can also use any extra time to return to items you marked as guesses. Don't change an answer on a hunch, but if you have new information or realize you misread the question, this is the time to change your answer.

4. Assuming there is no penalty for guessing, it is much better to guess than to leave any blanks. If it is blank, it is wrong. If it is answered, you have at least a 20 to 25% percent chance of getting it right—even without reading the question! If you can narrow it down to two, then you have a 50-50 chance!

5. Multiple choice questions are designed so that

each option is in itself a true-false question. Pencil in a "T", "F" or "?" next to each option to rule it in or out.

6. If you really want to make yourself anxious during a test, taking time to worry about missed questions is one way to accomplish that. But it won't help your performance, it will waste time, and it may interfere with thinking about questions to which you DO know the answer. This topic was addressed in Chapter 7, Self Talk and Anxiety Management.

7. Behavioral scientists will study almost anything. They actually have done research on whether it is a good idea to change your original answer on a test or not. Their conclusion: First responses tend to be correct. So—don't change your answer unless you remember something you didn't recall when you first answered the question—or if you get a clue from another question in the test. Clues from other test items are not likely on standard-ized exams but often happen on classroom tests.

8. Don't look for the exceptions to the rule. The instruc-tions usually state that you are to choose the "best" answer—so choose what is most generally true.

9. As you know by now, cramming is not an effective study method, and you probably won't be in very good physical condition for the exam.

10. Not a good idea. Last minute quizzing tends to make students over-anxious. Rather than ner-vously quizzing, it would be a better use of time to spend those few minutes getting mentally focused and prepared. Try saying something useful

to yourself such as, "I am going to use all the information I have studied," "I look forward to showing the teacher what I know," "I will use all my best test-taking skills today."

11. Marking (or making a mental note on computerized tests), key words in the question is an excellent test-taking skill. Ignoring a key word in either the stem or the option usually leads to an incorrect answer.

12. Know where you want to be at the halfway point of the time allowed (i.e., 30 minutes of a one-hour exam). Ideally you will be a little over halfway through the exam. On a paper-and-pencil test, you may want to leave yourself five to ten minutes at the end to check back over your work. On computer-based exams, reviewing answered items is not usually an option.

13. Good! Students often get tripped up when they forget they are looking for the "false" or "wrong" answer in negatively-worded questions.

14. Try to list or recall any facts that would rule an option in or out. Can you remember anything from your text, PowerPoint slides or notes? Can you sketch it out in the test margin or with your finger on the desk? Doing this sometimes reveals connections or information you really do know but are not thinking of in this context.

15. Look for clues, such as longer length or more detail in an option.

16. This is more likely to happen on a standardized

exam. If you find you must answer questions you don't have time to read, the best strategy is to fill in the "dots" straight down one column. Statistically, this strategy gives you a better chance of getting more items correct.

17. When you are able to figure out the reason you missed a question, it is much easier to prevent making the same type of error in the future. Was the information in your notes? Did you misread the question or an option? Did you run out of time when studying? Did you run out of time on the test?

18. Why make yourself sick? You will not be able to function at your best mentally, if you are not functioning well physically.

19. Spending too much time on one question can deprive you of the time needed for the rest of the exam. And remember that your first answer is most often the correct one.

20. If you have difficulty finishing classroom tests in the allotted time, you may have difficulty finishing the NCLEX and other standardized tests. When you have prepared thoroughly for an exam, you will be able to answer the questions more quickly and confidently.

Final Note: *Never* wait until the last few minutes of an exam to transfer all the answers to the answer sheet. Too many students have failed exams simply by running out of time or mis-marking the answer sheet as they raced to beat the clock. If you do mark answers on the test and then transfer them to the answer sheet, set up a system of doing that every 10 questions.

Score Interpretation — Test-Taking

65-80   Excellent test taking skills! Keep up the good work.

45-64   Good, but room for improvement.

Below 44   Let's get to work!

 # Goal: Become a Smart Test-Taker

Smart Test Taking

What a drag! You get a test back and see that you missed a couple of questions, not because you didn't know the topic, but because you made one of the many possible test-taking errors. The goal of this chapter is to make you test-wise. Never imagine, however, that being test-wise will by itself get you through nursing school.

Occasionally, you can pick up a point or two based on test-taking skills, but, fundamentally, knowledge of the subject is what leads to a good grade on a test. Still, why not get that extra point because you are an efficient test-taker? Here's an added bonus: knowing you are an efficient test-taker helps build confidence and relieve test anxiety as the test date looms.

Nursing Students' Tests

For nursing students, life sometimes seems to be one test after another. If you feel you live from test to test, or that you are always studying for one test or another, you're right. On average, nursing courses have a test every two to three weeks followed by a final exam. Given that students are enrolled in at least four courses with that testing schedule, and a semester is approximately fifteen weeks long, there can be as many as 24 tests each semester. That's a lot of tests! That's also a good reason to develop excellent test-taking skills as soon as possible.

Tests in nursing programs are likely to cover more information and to be more detailed than tests previously experienced by incoming students. Unlike previous exams, nursing school tests don't have many questions requiring only a general knowledge. Your instructors expect you to apply the information you have learned. In fact that is generally the favored testing method; to give you questions that require the application of information to a real-life health care problem.

Additional pressure comes from the fact that a nursing student must pass every course. Course failure may mean dropping the class or dropping out of the program and having to wait for a semester or even a year to return to school. Passing the course depends on passing the tests.

 Rationale

Preparing for Tests

The best way to deal with the pressure of exams is to have a comprehensive study system, like the one presented in this book. If you have prepared according to this system, you will find you can calmly pass all those tests, because you will have the detailed knowledge you gained by systematic reading, note-making and review. Following this system, you will have been over portions of the information in different ways at least eight times before you take the test. Count the ways: prereading, hearing the lecture, making rough notes during lecture, reading the printed materials (text and handouts), making your final set of notes, reviewing at least twice, and self-testing. You are now ready to show what you know!

Terminology for Objective Tests

Let's be sure we are using the same language when we talk about tests.

What most students call a "question," will here be referred to as an *"item."* An item includes the stem and all the response options.

When we use the word 'stem,' we mean the 'question' part of the test item. The stem asks you to choose one or more of the options as an answer. Stems can be worded either positively (a true response) or negatively (a false response). Stems may also include a clinical scenario preceding the directions or question.

'Response options' or *'alternatives'* are the possible answers to an objective test. You must choose one or more of them.

'Distractors' are incorrect answers. They are literally meant to distract you from the correct response, which is called the *'keyed option.'* A 'keyed option' is the one on the answer key.

Example

This Is The Stem:

The first thing a nurse should do when giving medication to a patient is:

Below Are the Response Options or Alternatives:

A. Read the label at least two times for instructions and contraindications
B. Wash hands
C. Be sure the medication is being given to the right person by checking the patient's ID bracelet
D. Be sure of the correct dosage

The *keyed option* is B. The problem here is that all of the options are good things to do. The clue in the stem is the word 'first.' Hand washing should precede any nursing procedure. A, C, and D are the distracters, because they are not "first."

The True-False Approach

You will not encounter true-false questions in your main class tests nor on the NCLEX, though some teachers may still use them for quizzes. But if you learn the 'true or false' approach, it will be helpful on all test item types because each option in multiple choice question is really a series of true-false questions.

True-false questions usually show the degree of relationship between two things, ideas or procedures. Given the information in the stem, you must decide if each option is true or false.

Following is a list of all possible responses to any true or false statement:

T = I know this is true
F = I know this is false
?T = I think this is true, but I'm not sure
?F = I think this is false, but I'm not sure
? = I haven't got a clue

Remember this list. You'll be using it a lot.

Strategies for the True-False Approach

After you read the true-false question (or options on a multiple-choice question), write your response in the margin next to the number or letter, according to the T, F, ?T, ?F, or ? system as described above.

> **Example**
>
> True ? or False ? *Frequency, urgency,* and *burning*
> on urination and the *presence of protein* in the urine
> are all symptoms of urethritis.

This statement is true if, and only if, all four underlined items are true of urethritis. In this case, 'presence of protein in the urine' is not, so, even though the rest of the stem is true, the item must be marked false.

The key here is to read the stem very carefully and underline (or make a mental note of) any word or phrase that can make an option either true or false.

If you have no idea if everything in the stem is true, guess, unless there is a penalty for guessing.

Your odds on guessing right are 50:50 on a true-false question, which is much better than receiving no credit for leaving the item blank.

Students tell us they have even found ways to use this system on computer tests, by using the fingers on one hand to represent the T, F, ? options as they consider each of the alternatives (a, b, c, d or 1, 2, 3, 4) depending on how the response options are labeled.

Types of Test Questions Used in Nursing School Exams

One Best Answer Multiple Choice Questions

This is probably the most common type of test item. In this type, there is a numbered stem and four or five lettered or numbered response options. Depending on the type of exam, you may have only one minute to read the whole item and select a response.

Remember that you are always looking for the *one*

best answer! Some response options may be sometimes, somewhat, somewhere true, but they may not be the one best answer, as in the following example.

Example

Directions: Choose the one best answer.

1. Corticosteroids:
    A. Must be used to treat fungal infections.
    B. Reduce inflammation.
    C. Can be used concurrently with aspirin without side effects.
    D. Are always used with patients who have infections.

Using our T, F,?T, ?F, or ? system, we can readily place an F in front of the A option and a T in front of the B option. Corticosteroids are used to treat inflammation, but fungal infections are typically treated with anti-fungal medications. C. and D. are problematic, because they are only sometimes true or true with only some patients.

Let's say you know that aspirin may be administered with corticosteroids, but there is a possibility of gastrointestinal bleeding or ulcers with some patients. Regarding D, corticosteroids could possibly mask signs of infection, so could be used only with caution in that case also. The one *best* answer that has no "ifs, ands, or buts" is B. This example shows why untrue options are called distracters, because they can lead down the side track of "this can be true sometimes." There is only one *best* answer!

Negatively-Worded Multiple Choice Questions

Negatively-worded multiple choice questions still require

the one best answer. Words in the stem that indicate the one false option is the keyed response include: "all…but," "all…except," "is not," "is not true of."

Example

All of the following statements about hemorrhoids are true *except:*

A. Hemorrhoids are clusters of vascular tissue and connective tissue.
B. Hemorrhoids are sometimes associated with portal hypertension.
C. Hemorrhoids are usually caused by an infection.
D. There are two main kinds of hemorrhoids: external and internal.

Three of these statements are true. You are looking for the one *false* statement. You will key (choose as your answer) the option you have marked with an F. Let's say you know that hemorrhoids involve vascular tissue in the anal canal. Given that, you might suspect C would be false, since clusters of vascular tissue and connective tissue are not necessarily associated with an infection. If C is false, it must be the one best answer, even if you are not so sure about B and D.

Using the T, F, ?T, ?F, ? system of notation will save you time if, on a paper-and-pencil exam, you have to leave an item unanswered and return to it later. You have left a record of your thoughts on your first pass through the item.

A word of warning: Don't choose an alternative you have marked (?) over one you have marked (?T). Some test takers have been known to pick an option about which they know absolutely nothing (?) instead of one they have some reason to think might be a good choice (?T).

Students tell us that, by a process of elimination, they can usually work a one best answer multiple choice item down to two options. For example, you have pared down the options to one marked T and one marked ?T. Now you can take time to examine every word in these two alternatives to see if there is anything that could possibly make one false. If you must guess between two options, your odds aren't bad: 50:50. When and if you must guess, please don't choose something questionably true (?T) over something you marked T.

Of course, if you read through the test and spot the one best answer immediately, just mark the keyed response and don't bother with working through all the options. Save the time for harder items.

One Best Response Clinical Vignette

This type of item is very popular in nursing school and may seem a bit strange to students who have not yet had patient contact. Don't let the clinical aspect rattle you. You will have been over the essential information in your studies. Clinical vignettes are popular, because they point up the relevance of your basic science education to clinical practice. The clinical vignette gives a thumbnail sketch of a patient's problem(s) and a set of answers to a particular question about that patient.

Example

A nurse is caring for a patient with congestive heart failure. His symptoms include an increase in blood pressure, cough, rales, weight gain, and neck and hand vein distention. What should the nurse suspect regarding this patient?

    A. Fluid volume deficit
    B. Fluid volume excess
    C. Diarrhea
    D. Insufficient IV fluid replacement

Tips for Answering: All the symptoms suggest extra fluid, so the answer certainly is not either A or D, because both imply insufficient fluids. Diarrhea, if severe, can lead to fluid volume deficit, for obvious reasons. By a process of elimination, it has to be B. Also, when you see two options that are identical except for one word (deficit vs. excess), a good guess is that one will be the keyed option.

Extended Matching

What distinguishes extended matching items from regular matching ones is, as the name indicates, there are more options. The options list can be very long. Also, the options are sometimes used for two or three different stems.

Example

Directions: Choose the best answer from the list of options below. Each answer may be used once, more than once, or not at all.

Have the patient close his eyes and then use a finger to hold one of his nostrils closed. Ask him to identify certain odors, such as peppermint or coffee. Which cranial nerve is assessed using this technique?

A. Cranial nerve I
B. Cranial nerve II
C. Cranial nerve III
D. Cranial nerve IV
E. Cranial nerve V
F. Cranial nerve VI
G. Cranial nerve VII
H. Cranial nerve VIII
I. Cranial nerve IX
J. Cranial nerve X
K. Cranial nerve XI
L. Cranial nerve XII

CHAPTER 8

Tips for Answering Extended Matching Questions

As you read the question, think of the possible answer before looking at the options. Then look for that answer in the options list. If you find it, mark the answer and move on. Approaching this type of item as a short-answer or fill-in-the blank saves time by allowing you to read the question only once and then skim for the answer among the response options.

If you don't find what you originally thought would be the keyed response, you'll have to go back to the question and reconsider what might fit the set of symptoms. Referring repeatedly back to the question can take a lot of time. There aren't many giveaways with extended matching questions, and the odds for guessing are not in your favor. Even so, never leave any item blank, unless there is a penalty for guessing. Did you choose A. Cranial nerve I?

Other Test-Taking Tips

Though these are not test item formats, some other types of questions that you will find on nursing exams may ask you to:

- **Prioritize** — in this type of question you may be asked what to do "first," "next," "immediately" or "initially."

    —Use the ABCs (airway, breathing, circulation) or Maslow's Hierarchy of Needs—often these types of questions will give you cues such as "which priority action" or "the highest priority."

    —Use the Nursing Process—use the steps in the nursing process to prioritize the action that needs to be taken.

- **Fill in the blank** — where you may be asked to perform a calculation, perhaps to ascertain the correct dosage of a medication.

- **Choose multiple responses** — this question type instructs you to select ALL the correct responses.

- **Use a figure or illustration** — data may be presented in a graphic form and you are asked to choose or point-and-click on the correct response.

In order to answer the question correctly, you must determine what the question is actually asking. The book *Successful Problem-Solving and Test-Taking for Beginning Nursing Students* or the updated version called *Test Question Logic (TQLogic) for Beginning Nursing Students* both by Patricia Hoefler offer practice in answering these types of questions.

Words of Wisdom on Taking Tests in General

Paper-and-pencil tests will typically be scored by optical scanning machines, so they will be accompanied by a scoring sheet with 'bubbles' where you will 'bubble in' the keyed option with a #2 pencil.

Computer versions of tests will usually require you to answer questions in a linear fashion, starting with question number one and answering each item, in order, through the entire exam. The computerized test may ask you to use an on-screen calculator, so scratch paper may not be allowed. Before the exam date, find out if the test will be paper-and-pencil or computer based, so you can plan your practice sessions and test-taking strategy accordingly.

The Day Before a Test

Think of test-taking as if it were a sport and yourself as a super-athlete at that sport. Before a competition, would you stay up all night? Eat unhealthy food? Overdose on caffeine (or any other drug)? Not if you wanted to win! Be sensible and take good care of your health—especially prior to major exams.

Assuming you are following the study system in this book, you will already have seen the information about eight times on the day before the test. You will probably need just one final review. Whether or not to self-test at this point depends on how much anxiety self-testing might create. If you would become a quivering mass of jelly, don't do it. You don't need that kind of aggravation. The study system taught in this book makes cramming unnecessary. Your knowledge and understanding of the information at this point should get you easily through the test, even when you have to make educated guesses. Stay positive!

During a Test

Keeping Track of the Time

When you first begin your test, take a minute to decide how much time you should spend (on average) per item and at what item number you should be at the half-way point of the time allowed for the test. If it is a paper-and-pencil exam, your calculation should allow five to ten minutes at the end to return to unanswered items to see if you need to guess or can make a more informed answer at that time. Thus, if you have 60 minutes to complete the test, and the test consists of 50 items, you can give yourself one minute per item and still have ten minutes to go back to unanswered items.

Exercise — Choose the One Best Answer

You have one hour to complete a 50-item multiple choice test. After 30 minutes, you should have reached item number:

A. 20
B. 30
C. 40
D. 50

The keyed option is B. You may not have answered each and every question during the first half. You need some time at the end to get back to unanswered items and either figure out the answer or, all else failing, guess, if there is no penalty for guessing.

Some items take less than a minute, some take more. But you should always stay close to the average as you work through the test and definitely get to the mid-point on time. In most tests, all the items have the same point value, so it is not advantageous to miss an easy item just because you spent too much time on a hard one.

If you are taking a paper-and-pencil exam, make an obvious check mark in the margin for any difficult item you decide to skip in the interest of time. The check mark will help you find this item quickly. Attentive test-takers often notice that some information or cue in a later item reminds them of the answer to an earlier item they skipped.

Cut Out Careless Error

Especially if you are using a Scantron® form, periodically check that the number you are "bubbling" corresponds to the test item you are answering. If you check every ten items, you'll have fewer bubbles to erase if you get off the numbering sequence. Just check that every time an item ends in zero, (10, 20, 30 etc.) the number on the answer sheet also ends in zero. Imagine your horror if you wait until the end and discover you are bubbling item 59 on a 60-item test! Even worse, that you got out of sync with the bubble sheet back at item 5! You will have to either power-erase and hope you have time to correct them all, beg the teacher on bended knee to let you fix the problem, or possibly fail the exam.

Do not try to be the first one out of the classroom after the test. On a paper-and-pencil exam, use any gift of time to:

- Double-check that your answer sheet numbers and test item numbers correspond.

- Double-check that all items are answered on the answer sheet.

- If you still have extra time, re-read any items that you guessed at earlier. You may find that you originally mis-read part of a stem or option.

- But DO NOT, and we repeat, DO NOT change answers on a hunch. More on this below.

Changing Answers

When you have plenty of time to go back over the test and re-read items already answered, you may be tempted to change an answer. Don't. Don't change an answer merely on a hunch. Your first guess is typically better than your second guess. But the research suggests that you may change your answer if you have a good reason, for example, some new information that makes your original response incorrect.

Expect the Unexpected

Sometimes, despite excellent preparation, you will encounter unexpected topics or question formats on an exam. Has your instructor always given 50-item exams until this one? Now there are 60 questions to answer in the same amount of time! What to do? The first thing to do is to take a deep breath. Anxiety will not help. (See Chapter 7, Self Talk and Test Anxiety.) Now is the time for productive self talk. Remind yourself that everyone else is in the same boat.

Concentrate on doing the best you can on each test item. Instead of using test time to ask your instructor about the unexpected changes, wait until after the test is over. And remember to use your professional communication skills. Stick to "I" statements rather than "you" statements. For example, rather than saying, "You wrote a confusing question, and you should not count it against us," try saying, "I found that question confusing, since the two concepts mentioned were so similar. Perhaps other students also found it confusing?"

Nine Tips for Improved Guessing on Classroom Exams

Unless there is a penalty for guessing, never leave any item unanswered. Penalties for guessing are rare, so you will probably be doing some guessing. If you have to guess, here are some suggestions for increasing the odds in your favor.

1. Don't choose a totally unfamiliar option. It's hard to believe, but some students choose an option about which they know absolutely nothing over another option that they know has at least some relationship to the key information in the stem.

2. Some form of repetition in the stem and option

points to a better guess. The repetition indicates some relationship. This is not always reliable, but, hey, it is a guess, isn't it?

"Eeny Meeny Miney Mo..."

Example

Directions: Select the one best answer.

In conducting a weight-loss program, what is the most accurate weight loss measure the nurse can use?

    A. Serum protein levels
    B. Calories ingested
    C. Carbohydrates ingested
    D. Daily weight measurements

You are looking for a similar word or phrase in the stem and in the option. Here the word "weight" and "measure" appear in both the stem and in option D, which is your best guess (and also correct).

---

3. Specific determiners and absolutes can eliminate options and improve odds on guessing.

"Always," "inevitably," "never," and "completely" are examples of absolutes and rarely describe anything in this world except death and taxes. When you see these descriptors you can usually rule out that option.

4. Grammatical errors can provide a hint. If, for example, the stem ends with 'an,' the beginning of any option has to be a vowel, not a consonant.

5. Just for fun, teachers sometimes throw in an absurd option, though this is unlikely occur on a standardized test.

Example

The body loses fluids by different routes. Which of the following is accurate?

A. Skin, by diffusion—500 ml
B. Skin, by perspiration—250 ml
C. Kidneys, by elimination—1500 ml
D. Expectoration—1000 ml

If you know that expectoration is spitting, you know D is *not* the keyed option.

---

6. Longer, more complicated, more complete options are more likely to be good guesses. Teachers sometimes put more information into the

keyed response in order to differentiate it from the distractors. The extra qualifiers or added information make it longer.

7. Familiarity breeds a good guess. If you recognize some relationship with parts of the option, or if it even sounds familiar in connection with the stem topic, it is better than a random guess. Don't choose an option that looks totally unfamiliar. After all, you have, at the very least, read the textbook and attended the lecture. Even if you haven't mastered the topic, it should sound familiar.

8. Guess one of two similar options, that is, two options that are identical except for one or two words.

Example

A hypertensive crisis is:
   A. A condition necessitating immediate increase in blood pressure
   B. A condition necessitating immediate decrease in blood pressure
   C. Not life threatening
   D. Does not require bed rest

Here, A and B are similar options. The only difference is in the words "increase" and "decrease." Even if you know nothing about hypertension, you will probably know from basic medical vocabulary that "hyper" means "too much" and would likely guess B. There is another giveaway in this item, again based on vocabulary alone. Any "crisis" is likely to be life-threatening, so that rules out option C. Another hint is that you probably shouldn't be running around if you have a medical crisis of any kind, thus eliminating D.

---

9. Especially in clinical scenarios that ask for a nursing response, a careful or conscientious answer is a good guess, if you have to guess. Keep in mind the ABCs, Maslow's hierarchy, patient safety and the Nursing Process.

If You Start Getting Tired During a Long Exam

Fatigue and hunger can lead to carelessness and leaving the exam early. To wake yourself from lethargy, try small exercises (that won't disturb your neighbors) like stretching your neck, raising your shoulders to your ears, making tight fists of your hands and releasing only after some tension builds. Tightening and then relaxing any muscle is refreshing. Exercising muscles in this way is not noisy and not very visible.

Find out if your teachers or exam proctors mind if you bring some energy-building food into the testing room, but avoid anything noisy (no carrot-chomping or crackling of paper, please). Nuts or dried fruits are a good choice and are easy to handle in the test situation. Better yet, eat a healthful meal immediately prior to the exam.

Out of Time

Finally, in the unlikely event that you run out of time on a classroom exam and must mark an answer without even reading the item, your best bet is to pick a single column and mark that column straight down to the end. You'll find you pick up more points by choosing one letter and just marking straight down. If you don't believe us, try it on an old exam answer sheet. Compare how many guesses are correct in the 'straight down the column' method versus random bubbling.

After A Test — It's Not Over Even When It's Over

Odds are that you missed a few items on the last test that you took. Learn from your mistakes! There is a great deal to discover when you are able to look over a graded exam. If you didn't do well on the exam you need to discover exactly what went wrong, so you can avoid making the same mistakes again. It may not be pleasant to look at test errors, but doing so can help you improve future test scores. Plan to attend the post-test review even if you made a good grade. Comments made during the review session can help you learn how test questions are chosen and that information will help you on future exams.

Did your lack of knowledge cause the error? If so, did you not have that information in your review notes? Why not? In our experience, this is the principle cause of missing points on tests.

Did you miss the item due to lack of test-taking skills? This is probably the second most frequent cause, especially carelessness in reading the item.

Were you so nervous that you didn't think straight during the exam? (See Chapter 7 on Self Talk.) Were you so physically ill that you couldn't function during the exam? Faculty usually have an alternative testing plan for a student who is seriously ill. Find out what it is before you need it!

Finally, do not let a bad test score side track you. What is done is done, and you must focus on the next exam. Do not let frustration derail your study plans. Look back over the previous chapter on Self Talk if you find yourself wasting energy on this unproductive type of thinking.

 **Intervention**

Exercise

Make some copies of the Test Error Analysis Worksheet (on the following page) to use after your next tests. After several analyses, you will have a very good idea of your main problem as a test-taker. Correct that problem, and show what you know on the next test!

✓ Evaluation

Check-Up on Test-Taking

What have you learned from this chapter that will improve your test-taking skills?

_____

_____

_____

_____

_____

_____

_____

_____

_____

Test Error Analysis Worksheet

Item # of question missed	Lack of knowledge? Yes / No	Was info in notes? Yes / No	Did you review the info? Yes / No	Did you self-test on the info? Yes / No	Was it a test-taking error? Yes / No	If yes, what type of test-taking error?

Worksheet 8.1

CHAPTER 8

📋 Summary

Since nursing students take so many exams, you need to become an excellent test-taker! Knowing the material well and using good test-taking strategies are the way to succeed.

Current Study Strategies

The next (and final) chapter deals with preparing for the NCLEX. Now that you have completed the main portion of this workbook, we'd like to ask you to take a few minutes and briefly describe your current study strategies in the space below. After completing this section you may wish to return to this same question in Chapter 1, on page 13. It will be interesting to discover the changes you have made in how you approach your studies!

_____

_____

_____

_____

_____

_____

_____

_____

_____

Student Feedback

When I don't change my test answers, I make better grades!

I am learning not to second guess myself.

When I am well prepared for an exam, I am much more confident!

I've discovered that sometimes I don't read the question carefully. Now I take time to make sure I know what it is asking before I answer it.

The last test I took was a really hard one, but I knew the information so well that I made an A! That experience really helped build my self confidence in using these new study skills.

 ## References

Fabrey, L.J., & Case, S.M. (1985). Further support for changing multiple-choice answers. *Journal of Medical Education, 60,* 488-491.

> Review of studies on changing answers on tests indicates that students should not change answers unless they have a good reason.

Hoefler, P.A. (2003). *Successful problem-solving & test-taking for beginning nursing students,* Burtonsville, MD: MEDS Publishing.

> This book is not just for beginning nursing students. It has many examples for students to work through as they learn to decipher what the question is "really" asking. It includes a CD-ROM.

Hoefler, P.A. (2005). *Test question logic (TQLogic) for beginning nursing students.* Burtonsville, MD: MEDS Publishing.

> This is an updated and re-titled version of the book listed above. It also includes a CD-ROM.

Pappworth, M.H. (1985). *Passing medical examinations.* London: Butterworths.

> General information on test-taking.

CHAPTER 8

Sides, M.B., & Korchek, N. (1998). *Successful test-taking.* (3rd ed.) Philadelphia: Lippincott.

Chapter 4 addresses test-taking techniques. Chapters 8-26 briefly review the essential information likely to be on nursing school tests.

Vital Skills

Preparing for the NCLEX-RN®

You've done it! You've graduated from nursing school. Now there's one more thing to do before you are allowed to begin your career as a Registered Nurse. The National Council Licensing Examination (NCLEX-RN®) is the test that all nurses must pass in order to be eligible for licensure. The exam is offered only as a computer-adaptive test. Therefore, if you are not familiar with computerized tests, part of your preparation will be to become comfortable with that format.

Plan Your Review Schedule

Depending on how much time you will have each week to devote to preparing for the NCLEX, you will probably need to begin your review two to four months before the exam date. Test preparation books and programs recommend 80 to 120 hours of study, review and practice questions. So, if you have twelve weeks to prepare, you will need to spend approximately 10 hours per week, if you have eight weeks to prepare, then you will need to spend approximately 15 hours per week, if you have six weeks you will need to spend about 20 hours per week, and so forth.

The NCLEX will provide another opportunity for you to use the category charts, flow charts and note cards you made for your classes. Since you created those notes and have studied from them before, they will make reviewing and remembering what was in those classes much easier than using all new study materials with which you are unfamiliar.

Arrange to take the exam as soon as is practical after completing your coursework. Taking the exam while still in "school mode" will help increase your likelihood of success. Most nursing programs strongly encourage students to take the NCLEX within one to three months of graduation. Save that "celebration vacation" until after the exam! If possible, wait until after the NCLEX to start your new job or increase your workload, if you've been working.

The National Council of State Boards of Nursing has an excellent website (www.ncsbn.org) that provides the information you will need for registering to take the exam.

Review Courses to Prepare for the NCLEX

The main advantage of review courses is that they force you to set aside time to prepare for the exam. If your program offers assistance in preparing for the NCLEX, by all means take advantage of it. But you will still need to plan your own review schedule. No general review course can possibly address the individual needs of each student. It is your job to continue to take charge of your learning and develop your own review schedule that will ensure you are fully prepared for the exam.

What to Review First

Performance on the NCLEX is highly correlated with grades in nursing courses. That tells you:

1. The content of nursing courses you have taken over the last two years will be on the NCLEX

2. How much you learned in those courses (and can still recall) will help you on the NLCEX

Begin planning your review schedule by looking back at the courses you have taken in nursing school. This will require some candid self assessment on your part. We recommend you begin your period of review with the topic that is most difficult for you (probably the one in which you received your lowest grade) and work towards the topics or areas that come more easily. This approach ensures that you will spend time on the areas that need the most work.

If you run out of time as you near the exam date, you'll be glad you didn't neglect your weaker areas to spend more time on your strong subjects. The point is to spend more time where you need the most review and spend less time where you need less review.

Students find some organ systems and medical specialties more complicated than others. The cardiovascular system, fluid and electrolyte balance, and renal function are often considered more difficult topics. Your prior knowledge of the subject and your level of personal interest make the order in which you review the topics a highly individual process.

You've labored long and hard toward your goal. Keep up the great work during this final phase!

Exit Exams

Many nursing programs administer an exit exam before students are allowed to take the NCLEX. There is a high correlation on many exit exams with performance on the NCLEX, which means if you perform well on the exit exam you are more likely to perform well on the NCLEX.

If your school gives an exit exam you may want to use the preparation strategies in this chapter to prepare for that exam. The results from the exit exam may then be used to help you focus your review and preparation strategies for the actual NCLEX.

Preparing For The NCLEX

The pages that follow will give you step-by-step instructions in how to prepare for the NCLEX. You may choose to use it as a checklist and mark the "Done" column as you complete each task.

A Step-byStep Guide to Preparing for the NCLEX

Step	Action to Take	Done
	Preparation	
1	Locate and organize your nursing text books and class notes by subject.	
2	Purchase or borrow one or two NCLEX review books with additional practice questions on CD-ROM. Many students say that they find the Saunders NCLEX review book to be the most helpful. *Note:* If you are still having difficulty discerning what some test questions are "really" asking, refer to the book *Successful Problem-Solving & Test-Taking for Beginning Nursing Students* by Patricia Hoefler. It's not just for beginning nursing students.	
3	Make a list of every nursing course and the grade received (and test grades, if you have that information.) Based on this information, list areas to review. Begin with the one that needs the most work (i.e., has the lowest grade), second is the next lowest and so on). Or, you may want to use the results from your exit exam. The results from that exam should give you an excellent idea of the areas that need more of your attention.	
4	Use your personal calendar to choose an exam date. Preferably within three months of graduation.	
	Schedule Review Time	
5	On your review/study calendar, mark off any dates you cannot study between the start of your review and the exam date.	
6	Beginning with the exam date, count **backwards** the number of days available between the start of review and testing date. How many hours on each of those days will you be able to study? Will that add up to the 80-120 hours recommended? If not, you may need to reschedule the exam date. Remember that the sooner you take the exam after graduation, the better. Make sure you leave the week (or at least five days) prior to the exam open, with nothing scheduled. This will allow time for a general review of the material and will give you a little "flex time" in case an emergency arises that gets you off track for a day or two.	

Continued

A Step-by-Step Guide to Preparing for the NCLEX

Step	Action to Take	Done
	Actual Review	
7	Estimate the time you will allocate to each topic, allowing time to go over some areas again near the end. Use the recommended 80-120 hours of review as a general guideline when planning your schedule. The activities that will be included in your review sessions for each topic will vary, but should permit you to: 1. Review your old charts, cards and other notes. 2. Take a 100-item NCLEX practice test. 3. Read and make study notes on any content material not yet mastered. 4. Self test over your own notes. 5. Answer short sets of NCLEX practice questions. 6. Review responses to practice questions. 7. Determine if topic is mastered (85% or higher on practice questions and self tests). If a topic is not yet mastered, write the name of the topic on a "Final Review List." 8. Repeat steps above as time allows and then move on to the next topic. The CD that accompanies many of the review books will give you feedback on the type of question and content area. We suggest that you create a tracking grid to record the topics that have been reviewed and learned to the 85% criterion.	
8	Once you have estimated the time you want to spend on each topic, re-count how many days and hours your review schedule allows. Is it enough? Do you need to change the start date for your review or the test date?	

Continued

A Step-by-Step Guide to Preparing for the NCLEX

Step	Action to Take	Done
	Actual Review	
9	On your calendar or schedule write for each day: • topics to review, • amount of time (hours) for each, • the score of your practice exams—by subject area. Once you have reached at least 85% mastery of the content, move on to the next topic. If you have used all the time that you allowed for that topic, you will need to either adjust your schedule to borrow a few hours from another topic and spend a little more time on that area now, or plan to add it to your "Final Review List" and come back to it during your final review in the week before the exam. *Suggestion:* It's probably better to move on and not get bogged down in one area, unless it is absolutely fundamental to everything else you will be studying.	
10	In addition to the daily quizzes you will be taking, plan to space at least three or four full-length practice tests (100+ questions) throughout your review period. This will let you know how effective your study/review system is and will still allow adequate time to remediate any areas that need further work. Schedule your last full-length practice test one or two weeks before the actual exam. You will continue to study, review and self-test during those last two weeks, but do not plan to take a full length practice test the last several days before the NCLEX. You don't need "test-taking burnout."	

How to Use Practice Questions
and Practice Exams

As a general rule, you will answer practice questions only after you have reviewed a topic. Using questions as your main review tool will not provide the structure necessary to pinpoint how to best spend your time. Most review books have short (10-20) sets of questions that are well-suited for self-testing. The longer tests (50-200 questions) should be used as practice exams and taken once or twice a week during your review period. Some exam preparation programs recommend that by the time you sit for the actual NCLEX, you should have answered 2,000-3,000 NCLEX-type questions.

 **Case Study**

Nicole is in her final semester of nursing school. She will graduate with a bachelor of science in nursing (BSN) in only a few weeks.

She has been using our study system since her first semester of nursing school and has a well-organized set of study notes to use as she begins preparing for the NCLEX.

Nicole has kept a record of her course grades (as well as individual exam scores for each course) so she knows where she needs to begin. She uses her list of course grades to help her decide which area will need the most review.

Nicole received her lowest grades during the first semester of the nursing program, while she was learning to adjust to the pace and the amount of material she was expected to learn. Since she received her lowest grade in Pharmacology, she lists this as the first area she will review. She will pay particular attention to the topics that were covered in the first semester of this multi-semester course.

Semester I Courses	Final Course Grade
Health History and Physical Assessment	88%
Pathophysiology I	83%
Adult Health Care	84%
Pharmacology I	80%
Fundamentals of Nursing	89%
Semester II Courses	
Pathophysiology II	88%
Community Health	95%
Nursing Care of Families with Children	91%
Medical Surgical Nursing	88%
Mental Health Nursing	93%
Semester III Courses	
Care of the Childbearing Family	93%
Pharmacology II	90%
Nursing Research	95%
Medical Surgical Nursing II (Theory)	89%
Medical Surgical Nursing II (Clinical)	96%
Semester IV Courses	
Synthesis of Nursing Knowledge	94%
Nursing as a Profession Seminar	93%
Nurse as Manager	90%
Medical Surgical Nursing III	92%

The next subject that Nicole lists is Pathophysiology. She was among the many students who struggled with the concept of fluid and electrolyte balance, so that will be at the top of her list of topics to review in patho. One of her teachers pointed out that given the current diabetes epidemic, she could count on seeing several questions about diabetes on the NCLEX exam, so diabetes will be next on her list of things to review in patho. Finally, she knows that cardiovascular disease is likely to be addressed on the NCLEX, so that is the third main area on which she will focus.

Nicole will also review much of what was covered the first semester in Adult Health Care. These three courses continued through other semesters, and Nicole was able to master much of the later material, but she knows this is her chance to review and fill in some gaps in her knowledge from those first difficult months of nursing school.

She has already purchased two highly-recommended NCLEX review books. She chose the ones that the students in the class ahead of her said were even harder than the actual NCLEX!

Scheduling

Next, Nicole gets out her calendar, so she can plan her review schedule and choose a date to take the NCLEX. The job she plans to accept will begin two months after graduation. She and her husband are planning a well-deserved vacation after she takes the NCLEX and before her new job begins. That leaves her about six weeks between graduation and the start of her vacation.

Graduation is on May 15 so she looks at her calendar and counts forward to the date her new job will begin, which is July 10. Now, counting backward from July 10 she blocks out three days to get settled back in and rest after her vacation. Continuing to count backwards she writes a "V" on the eight days she and her husband will be out of town.

The next decision Nicole makes is how many days there should be between the date she takes the NCLEX and when they leave for their vacation. She decides that two days after the exam should give her plenty of time to get ready, so she counts back two days from the start of her vacation and writes a "P" on those two days. The "P" stands for preparation.

She then writes NCLEX lightly on her calendar. Now she has to figure out if she's left herself enough time to cover all the topics before she takes the exam.

CHAPTER 9

Nicole has already decided which courses and notes need to be reviewed. The review books indicate that she should spend between 80 and 120 hours in review and self-test in order to be well prepared. She thinks that it is realistic to study for about six hours per day, five days a week. If she puts in 30 hours per week, then she needs to schedule four weeks of study.

So, counting backwards from the tentative NCLEX date, she lands on the date of her graduation ceremony. Many of Nicole's family and friends are coming to her graduation and there are at least two parties over the weekend that she plans to attend, so she knows either the NCLEX date or her study schedule will have to change.

Nicole sees that if she studies on two of the three Saturdays before the exam, she will be able to stick to her original NCLEX test date.

The scheduling is pretty tight, and she does not have much flexibility in how she will spend her time if any emergencies arise. After talking with her nursing school advisor, Nicole decides to spend eight hours a day studying for the first two weeks, in addition to studying on Saturdays, so she can build in a little bit of a cushion.

Nicole is busy planning for her pinning ceremony and graduation, and she knows she will not be able to do much (if any) studying before graduation, but with the advance work she has done, she will be ready to dive right into reviewing the material immediately after the celebrations are over.

Study and Review Begin

Nicole had a wonderful graduation weekend and is now starting her first day of study and review. She has drawn up a chart entitled "Final Review List" on which she will keep a record of any area that she does not receive at least an 85% when she begins self testing.

Once graduation is over, Nicole calls the testing center to schedule the exam. Because she is calling several weeks in advance, Nicole is able to arrange to take the NCLEX on the date she has chosen.

Nicole had already identified Pharmacology as the subject to review first and has gathered her charts from the first semester. She can tell that some of them are not complete, so her first task is to update her charts so they contain all the information she needs to master. She uses her course textbook, the class handouts and the review books to fill in the gaps in her charts. It's slow going and takes most of the morning. Nicole is a little discouraged. She decides to use productive self-talk and reminds herself that once she has re-worked her charts the rest will come more easily.

At the end of day one, Nicole has nearly finished updating her notes. She writes a "to do" list for tomorrow so she can get started quickly on the work. Finally, she pulls out her "NCLEX Study Hours" tracking grid and records that she has studied for eight hours today. Whew! A good start.

At the end of the first week Nicole is on track and feeling good about the progress she has made. Today she plans to take her first practice exam using the CD that came with a review book. This will be a 100 question exam and she is looking forward to seeing how well she does on the questions.

The score that she receives on the practice exam is a 70%, which is lower than she had expected. Nicole decides to examine the types of questions that she answered incorrectly. She discovers that the items she missed were mostly from topics she had not yet studied. That was good news! When she counted up the items relating only to the topics she had studied her score increased to 87%. Much better.

By the end of the third week Nicole has studied and reviewed each of the topics thoroughly. She is ready to spend the last week reviewing and self-testing in the areas she feels need a little more work. She has taken one or two full length practice exams each week during her preparation for the NCLEX, as well as short paper-and-pencil quizzes over the topics.

Final Review Time

In order to determine what areas still need work, she looks over her "Final Review List" and also takes another full length practice exam on the computer. This one has 200 questions, so it will be a test of her endurance as well as her knowledge of the material.

This will probably be her last full length practice exam, as she does not want to experience test-taking burn-out prior to the big day of the NCLEX.

Nicole has learned that there are really two parts to taking the NCLEX. The first, and most important part, is learning the material thoroughly. The second part is learning to answer the question that the test item is asking, and not "read into" the question.

On the day before she is scheduled to take the NCLEX, Nicole begins the last phase of her preparation, the mental and the physical. She plans her meals for maximum nutrition and, even though she is feeling a little nervous, she will not skip any meals.

Nicole spends the day in light review and does not do any self testing. She goes for a nice, long walk mid-day and takes a hot bath at bedtime to help her relax. Nicole sets two alarm clocks and places them far from the bed so she will have to get up to turn them off. No chance of oversleeping tomorrow! And throughout the day she has been using productive self-talk to remind herself how well-prepared she is for the NCLEX.

Taking the NCLEX

On the morning of the NCLEX exam, Nicole eats an especially nutritious breakfast, with plenty of protein and complex carbohydrates, and allows an extra half hour for her drive to the testing center. When she arrives at the testing center she is feeling a little nervous, but decides to channel that feeling into eagerness to show what she has learned. Nicole knows she is well-prepared and looks forward to her future as a Registered Nurse.

NCLEX Content and Format

Distribution of the Content

The NCLEX is an application-based test, which means you must apply basic science concepts to clinical situations. It is organized by the broad theme of "meeting clients' needs". The four major areas of the exam are:

- Physiological Integrity
- Safe and Effective Care Environment
- Health Promotion and Maintenance
- Psychosocial Integrity

You will be expected to analyze the information you have been learning for the last two (or more) years and apply it to clinical situations.

Make sure you have familiarized yourself with the most current list of topics and requirements issued by the National Council of State Boards of Nursing by visiting their website, www.ncsbn.org.

NCLEX Test Format

The NCLEX is administered using a computer-adaptive testing format. What that means is how you answer each test item will determine the level of difficulty of the next test item. The length of the exam is determined by the size of the sample that the software program requires to accurately determine the extent of your knowledge. The time limit for the entire exam is six hours, though most students say they are able to finish in about four hours. Currently the maximum number of exam questions is 265 and the minimum is 75.

No matter how many test questions you are given, 15 of them will be experimental items that are being tested for use in future exams. All standardized exams test future questions in this manner. These items will not count either for or against you in determining whether or not you pass the exam. But since you will not be told which questions are experimental, you must answer each question to the best of your ability.

The NCLEX will end when one of the following events has taken place:

- The six hour time limit or the 265 question limit has been reached,
- You have answered at least 75 questions and have passed the exam,
- You have answered at least 75 questions and have not passed the exam.

The best strategy to use for this exam is to be well-prepared in terms of content and be familiar with answering NCLEX-type questions on the computer—in that order.

To mentally prepare yourself, the best strategy is—plan to be at the testing center for the full six hours and plan to answer all 265 questions.

Test Time

The Day Before the Exam

As noted in our case study, the best way to spend the day before the NCLEX is a combination of light review, good nutrition, moderate exercise and a full night's rest—with a back-up alarm clock set, so there's no chance of over-sleeping.

The Day of the Exam

After a good night's rest and a nutritious breakfast, plan to arrive at the testing center twenty to thirty minutes before your scheduled exam time. This will allow time for traffic delays on the way, and, once you arrive, will give you a few minutes to do some deep breathing exercises, make a bathroom stop and whatever else you need to do to finish preparing yourself mentally and physically.

Although you will not be allowed to carry anything into the exam room, you should plan to dress in a way that you will not be too hot or too cold, so you can fully concentrate on answering questions. Many test centers are notorious for being uncomfortably over air-conditioned, especially in the summer months.

Most testing centers offer a number of standardized exams, such as those required for admission to law school, medical school or graduate school, so do not assume that the other people in the room with you are taking the NCLEX.

Examine your work station before you begin the exam. Make sure you can easily see the computer screen and that your chair is a comfortable height. If you have any computer difficulties during the exam, contact the room monitor or proctor immediately. They will need to make a report of anything that does not go according to the standards set by the testing committee.

Instead of offering paper and pencil for students to use during standardized tests, many testing centers now provide a small white board and marker. Find out which your testing center offers so you can use the same thing when taking practice NCLEX exams. You want to closely simulate the actual conditions, so they will all be familiar to you on test day.

No matter how well you prepare, some unexpected topic or subject matter may be presented. If it is, use deep breathing and productive self talk to remain calm. Remind yourself that you are well prepared for this exam and will continue to focus on the questions in front of you.

"After all the study and review, the NCLEX
seemed pretty easy!"

If An Emergency Arises

Despite your best efforts, an emergency or other unforeseen event may occur on test day. If you are feeling ill, if you have a car accident or if you receive upsetting news as you walk out the door, it's time to re-think your testing strategy.

Even though you will probably have to pay for the already scheduled exam, nursing faculty members say they advise students that it is much better to reschedule the NCLEX than to try and "gut it out" and take the test when physically ill or emotionally upset.

If an emergency does occur, call the exam center to let them know you will not be coming. Do what you can to remedy the situation and reschedule the exam as soon as possible.

 ## Summary

At the beginning of this workbook we told you the secret to success. Remember?

Success = System + Schedule

Scheduling enough time and mastering the material in a systematic way will lead to success. The formula applies not only to preparing for the NCLEX; it will also apply to the other examinations you will be taking throughout your career, so refer back to this chapter (and book) as needed.

 ## Student Feedback

After all the studying and reviewing I did, the NCLEX seemed pretty easy!

I took my time and answered the NCLEX questions the best I could, and before I knew it, it was over. And, yes, I passed!

The NCLEX was exactly like you said it would be! Right down to the freezing-cold testing center. These strategies were so useful in helping me do well.

I was able to say positive things to myself all during the exam.

That really helped me stay on track and do well, even when I started getting tired.

When you know you are well prepared, it really helps with your confidence!

The strategies taught here really helped - not only during my courses, but also for the NCLEX. Thanks!

 # References

Hoefler, P.A. (2005). *Test question logic (TQLogic) for beginning nursing students.* Burtonsville, MD: MEDS Publishing.

> This book is not just for beginning nursing students. It has many detailed examples for students to work through as they learn to decipher what the question is "really" asking. Includes a CD-ROM.

National Council of State Boards of Nursing. Retrieved from http://www.ncsbn.org

> The developers of the NCLEX. Has all the current registration and testing requirements.

Sides, M.B., & Korchek, N. (1998). *Successful test-taking.* (3rd ed.) Philadelphia: Lippincott.

> Chapter 4 addresses test-taking techniques. Chapters 8-26 briefly review various topics and include reasoning exercises.

Silvestri, L.A. (2005). *Saunders comprehensive review for the NCLEX-RN examination.* Philadelphia: Elsevier Saunders.

> A comprehensive book of review questions and answers divided into subtopics.

Waterhouse, J.K., & Beeman, P.B. (2003). Predicting NCLEX-RN success: Can it be simplified? *Nursing Education Perspectives,* Vol. 24, 1, pp. 35-39.

> NCLEX results are highly correlated with course grades. Authors could accurately identify risk by counting the number of Cs, or lower, earned in nursing courses.

Looking Forward!

Thank you for allowing us to join you on your way to becoming a licensed RN!

We trust that the strategies presented in *Vital Skills* have been helpful and will continue to serve you in the future.

Students and professionals who are prepared for the tasks ahead of them, who create order and organization in their work, and who remained engaged in the process of learning are unstoppable!

We would enjoy hearing from you. We would especially like to hear how you are using the information presented here and how you are progressing toward your goals. Do you have any specific questions with which we can help? Have you made any charts that are particularly useful? Have you come across some recent research that will help us improve the study techniques that we teach?

You may contact us via our website at www.vitalstudyskills.com

We wish you all the best in your future endeavors.

Looking Forward,

—Kathleen C. Straker
—Eugenia G. Kelman

About the Authors

Kathleen Straker, M.Ed., has worked in nursing education and medical education for two decades. The study skills workshops she teaches have helped numerous students graduate to careers in nursing, medicine and research. Ms. Straker is President of The Straker Group, LLC, a consulting firm based in Houston, Texas. This is her second book.

Eugenia Kelman, Ph.D., is a cognitive-behavioral psychologist. She has served on the faculty and in the administration at Colorado State University in Ft. Collins, CO; The University of Texas Medical Branch, Galveston, TX and at Cornell University in Ithaca, NY. Her favorite question is, "What can I learn from this?"

About the Illustrator

Tammy Dubinsky grew up in the small town of Ardrossan, Alberta Canada. It was here that her mom taught her how to draw apple trees and barbed wire fences in proper perspective. Tammy graduated from the Alberta College of Art & Design, where she received a Bachelor of Design, majoring in Visual Communication. She gives credit to her classmates and instructors for being her biggest inspiration. Currently she attends the Vancouver Film School and is pursuing a diploma in classical animation. Tammy loves to draw and is very grateful to be able to do it for a living.

www.VitalStudySkills.com